BAYLOR

DAILY DEVOTIONS FOR DIE-HARD FANS

BEARS

BAYLOR

Daily Devotions for Die-Hard Fans: Baylor Bears
© 2014, 2015 Ed McMinn
Extra Point Publishers; P.O. Box 871; Perry GA 31069

Cover design by John Powell and Slynn McMinn
Interior design by Slynn McMinn

Every effort has been made to identify copyright
holders. Any omissions are unintentional. Extra Point
Publishers should be notified in writing immediately
for full acknowledgement in future editions.

BEARS

Daily Devotions for Die-Hard Fans
Available Titles

ACC
Clemson Tigers
Duke Blue Devils
FSU Seminoles
Georgia Tech Yellow Jackets
North Carolina Tar Heels
NC State Wolfpack
Virginia Cavaliers
Virginia Tech Hokies

BIG 10
Michigan Wolverines
Ohio State Buckeyes
Penn State Nittany Lions

BIG 12
Baylor Bears
Oklahoma Sooners
Oklahoma State Cowboys
TCU Horned Frogs
Texas Longhorns
Texas Tech Red Raiders

SEC
Alabama Crimson Tide
More Alabama Crimson Tide
Arkansas Razorbacks
Auburn Tigers
More Auburn Tigers
Florida Gators
Georgia Bulldogs
More Georgia Bulldogs
Kentucky Wildcats
LSU Tigers
Mississippi State Bulldogs
Missouri Tigers
Ole Miss Rebels
South Carolina Gamecocks
More South Carolina Gamecocks
Texas A&M Aggies
Tennessee Volunteers

NASCAR

Daily Devotions for Die-Hard Kids
Alabama, Auburn, Georgia
Available in 2015: Baylor, Texas, Texas A&M for Kids

---

www.die-hardfans.com

BAYLOR

DAILY
DEVOTIONS
FOR
DIE-HARD
FANS

BEARS

IN THE BEGINNING

Read Genesis 1, 2:1-3.

"God saw all that he had made, and it was very good" (v. 1:31).

The Baylor faculty was not the least bit interested in an intercollegiate "rugby modified" team, but the students persisted until, in 1899, the Baylor Bulldogs took the field. Football had arrived.

Alan J. Lefever relates in *The History of Baylor Sports* that the first documented football game at Baylor occurred on Thanksgiving Day in 1895. It was little more than a few students getting together for an afternoon of horsing around since it featured the men of Georgia Burleson Hall and the members of the R.C.B. Calliopeans Club. (Burleson won 24-4.) The game wasn't even called football, but rather "rugby modified."

Whatever it was, this new sport was spreading rapidly across the nation's campuses. In 1896, the Baylor student body asked the faculty to allow a team to compete intercollegiately. The faculty declined; they felt the students were being "too hasty." That didn't discourage the students. They assembled a petition signed by every male student and presented their request again in 1897. They ran into the same stone wall.

The faculty couldn't stop the Baylor men from playing what amounted to intramural football games, however. These garnered such widespread interest and became so popular that the faculty relented in 1899.

BEARS

History sketchily records that the first Baylor football team went 2-1-1 with two games against Toby's Business College and one each against Texas A&M and TCU. The loss was to A&M.

The first games were played on campus at an area known as the West End, which probably doubled as the baseball field and the parade ground for the school's military units. It had a grandstand that would seat about 1,000 people. The original mascot was a Bulldog (its origin unknown), but it was soon dropped.

However humble it may have been, Baylor football had begun.

Beginnings are important, but what we make of them is even more important. Consider, for example, how far the Baylor football program has come since that first season. Every morning, you get a gift from God: a new beginning. God hands to you as an expression of divine love a new day full of promise and the chance to right the wrongs in your life. You can use the day to pay a debt, start a new relationship, replace a burned-out light bulb, tell your family you love them, chase a dream, solve a nagging problem . . . or not.

God simply provides the gift. How you use it is up to you. People often talk wistfully about starting over or making a new beginning. God gives you the chance with the dawning of every new day. You have the chance today to make things right – and that includes your relationship with God.

By 1900, there is evidence Baylor men were facing off against other institutions in baseball, basketball, golf, football, track & field, and tennis.
— Alan J. Lefever

Every day is not just a dawn; it is a precious chance to start over or begin anew.

THE PANIC BUTTON

Read Mark 4:35-41.

"He said to his disciples, 'Why are you so afraid? Do you still have no faith?'" (v. 40)

That first swing from Texas Tech hit Baylor like a Mike Tyson right cross." A lesser team would have panicked, but these were the Bears of 2013.

On Nov. 16, Art Briles' Bears rumbled into Arlington to take on the Red Raiders. With a 7-3 record, Tech presented a formidable challenge for Baylor, which was flying high. The Bears went into the game 8-0 and ranked fifth in the Bowl Championship Series standings. They were gunning for their first Big 12 title.

So Tech came out of the locker room and took a 14-0 lead before the fans had even warmed their seats. For Baylor, "the defense looked lost. The offense sputtered." It was the first time all season the team had trailed by more than a touchdown.

With so much pressure sitting on their shoulders, the boys from Waco could well have panicked and gotten themselves in more trouble. "We knew this was going to be a dogfight," Briles said, apparently not at all surprised at being behind. But the Bears shrugged their shoulders and answered with a quick score. Junior quarterback Bryce Petty, the NCAA's passing efficiency leader, hit junior receiver Levi Norwood with a 40-yard touchdown pass.

Tech wasn't through, though, scoring quickly and then forcing a Baylor punt. Perhaps *now* was an appropriate time for a little panic to settle in. Not at all. The defense held and Norwood returned the punt 58 yards for a touchdown.

By halftime, the calm and collected Bears led 35-27 on their way to a 63-34 romp that never showed even a hint of panic.

Have you ever experienced that suffocating sensation of fear escalating into full-blown panic? Maybe it was the awful time when you couldn't find your child at the mall or at the beach. Or the heartstopping moment when you realized that the vehicle speeding right toward you wasn't going to be able to stop.

As the story of the disciples and the storm illustrates, the problem with panic is that it debilitates us. While some of them were landlubbers unaccustomed to bad weather on the water, the storm panicked even the professional fishermen among them into helplessness. All they could do was wake up an exhausted Jesus.

We shouldn't be too hard on them, though, because we often make an even more grievous mistake. They panicked and turned to Jesus; we panic and often turn away from Jesus by underestimating both his power and his ability to handle our crises.

We have a choice when fear clutches us: We can assume Jesus no longer cares for us, surrender to it, and descend into panic, or we can remember how much Jesus loves us and resist fear and panic by trusting in him.

It's impressive when you're down 14-0 and 20-7 and withstand that surge against a good team and finish like we did.
     — Art Briles on the Bears' lack of panic vs. Texas Tech

To plunge into panic is to believe — quite wrongly
— that Jesus is incapable of handling
the crises in our lives.

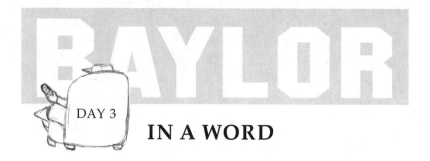

IN A WORD

Read Matthew 12:33-37.

*"For out of the overflow of the heart the mouth speaks.
The good man brings good things out of the good stored
up in him, and the evil man brings evil things out of the
evil stored up in him" (vv. 34b-35).*

Kim Mulkey had thirty seconds to say something that would rescue her team's national title hopes. She said it.

It was a simple timeout. It was just that everything was riding on it. Baylor's head coach had called it because a glorious season was on the verge of getting washed right down the drain.

On April 3, 2005, the 31-3 Lady Bears met LSU in the national semifinals, and the Texas women were in real big trouble. With 7:40 left in the first half, LSU led 24-9. "We're getting embarrassed on national television," Mulkey muttered to her assistants. ESPN's commentators agreed, describing what was happening as an avalanche and a burial.

So Mulkey called a timeout. What could she say? She could have told the stark truth: LSU was ranked number one and only once in the history of the women's Final Four had a team come back from a 15-point deficit and won.

But Mulkey first said nothing; she simply smiled, a "look of confidence, almost cockiness." Then she talked. She delivered a three-pronged message: 1) relax; 2) remember the season opener when they had mounted a furious comeback against this same team before losing by only one point; and 3) switch to a zone.

The players listened, "and as if on cue, [they] rediscovered their groove." Chelsea Whitaker hit a fast-break layup late in the first half to complete a 19-4 run that tied the game at halftime. LSU never recovered, losing 68-57.

A blowout of Michigan State completed the run to the title, kept alive by a few words spoken during a 30-second timeout.

These days, everybody's got something to say and, likely as not, a place to say it. Talk has really become cheap as the 24-hour media scramble to fill their programming with just about anyone who is willing to expound on just about anything.

But words still have power, and that includes not just those of the talking heads, hucksters, and pundits on television, but ours also. Our words are perhaps the most powerful force we possess for good or for bad. The words we speak today can belittle, wound, humiliate, and destroy. They can also inspire, heal, protect, and create. Our words both shape and define us. They also reveal to the world the depth of our faith.

We should never make the mistake of underestimating the power of the spoken word. After all, speaking the Word was the only means Jesus had to get his message across – and look what he managed to do.

We must always watch what we say because others sure will.

We were getting ripped and chewed, but in that timeout she laid it on the table for us.
— Guard Jordan Davis on the first-half timeout vs. LSU

Choose your words carefully; they are the most powerful force you have for good or for bad.

GIFT-WRAPPED

Read James 1:13-18.

"Every good and perfect gift is from above, coming down from the Father of the heavenly lights" (v. 17).

Teams are accustomed to receiving gifts from the bowl games in which they play, but the Bears once were handed a memento that -- well, it wasn't anything to write home to momma about.

From 1948-61, the Baylor program made its first-ever bowl run, appearing in six post-season games. The '48 team went 6-3-2 and made the program's first bowl appearance, beating Wake Forest 20-7 in the Dixie Bowl in Birmingham, Ala.

Head coach George Sauer's first team in 1950 went 7-3 and landed in the school's first-ever "major" bowl, a 17-14 loss to Georgia Tech in the Orange Bowl. The 7-3 squad of 1954 played in the Gator Bowl in Jacksonville.

Only nine points separated the 1956 team from an unbeaten season in head coach Sam Boyd's first season in Waco. The Bears were heavy underdogs to Tennessee in the Sugar Bowl and pulled off a 13-7 upset. The 1960 team made it to No. 7 in the polls before dropping a pair of close games and finishing 8-2. The prize was a return trip to the Gator Bowl.

And then there was the 1961 Gotham Bowl. Injuries decimated the '61 Bears, and they struggled to a 5-5 record. The sponsors of this new bowl game in New York were desperate to find teams to play, having failed to secure a match-up for a game in 1960. The

Bears accepted an invitation and beat Utah State 24-9.

The bowl was plagued by mismanagement and poor planning from the start and lasted only two years. A good example of the problems is the gift the Baylor players received. At the last minute, someone informed the bowl's novice promoters that custom called for the bowl to present gifts to the players and coaches as mementoes of the occasion. So they scurried around and came up with a special gift indeed for everyone: a shoeshine kit.

Receiving a gift is nice, but giving has its pleasures too, doesn't it? The children's excitement on Christmas morning. That smile of pure delight on your spouse's face when you came up with a really cool anniversary present. Your dad's surprise that time you didn't give him a tie or socks. There really does seem to be something to this being more blessed to give than to receive.

No matter how generous we may be, though, we are grumbling misers compared to God, who is the greatest gift-giver of all. That's because all the good things in our lives – every one of them – come from God. Friends, love, health, family, the air we breathe, the sun that warms us, even our very lives are all gifts from a profligate God. And here's the kicker: He even gives us eternal life with him through the gift of his son.

What in the world can we possibly give God in return? Our love and our life.

From what we get, we can make a living; what we give, however, makes a life.

— *Arthur Ashe*

Nobody can match God for giving, but you can give him the gift of your love in appreciation.

LANGUAGE BARRIER

Read Acts 2:1-21.

"Divided tongues, as of fire, appeared among them, and a
tongue rested on each of them. All of them were filled with
the Holy Spirit and began to speak in other languages, as
the Spirit gave them ability" (vv. 3-4 NRSV).

The recruit wasn't too sure Baylor would be the right place for
him. After all, he couldn't understand half of what the head coach
was saying.

After left tackle Jason Smith's departure to the pros following
the 2008 season, Art Briles and his staff found a most unusual
replacement. He was Danny Watkins, and he came to Baylor from
Butte College in Northern California. At 6'3" and 310 lbs., Watkins
had the requisite size; he also had an occasional mean streak.

Briles hadn't played much football, but he had a good excuse:
He was Canadian. He had grown up playing hockey and rugby.
When he arrived in Waco, he was 24 years old and had more
experience as a firefighter than he did playing football.

Watkins' first conversation with Briles left him unsure about
Baylor, but his indecision had nothing to do with football. "I
talked to Coach Briles on the phone for about 30 minutes, and
honestly, I don't think I understood half of what he said," Watkins
recalled. "And I'm not sure he understood me, either."

Only when Watkins visited the campus did the language barrier start to crumble. Even after he arrived and started practicing,

however, communication was sometimes difficult. Pleased with his progress, the coaches kept telling him, "Good job, Danny! That dog will hunt." Perplexed, Watkins finally tapped his left guard on the shoulder and asked, "Where's this dog they keep talking about?"

A two-year starter, Watkins was taken 23rd in the 2011 draft.

As Danny Watkins' career shows, language often erects a barrier to understanding. Recall your overseas vacation or the call to a tech support number when you got someone who spoke English but didn't understand it. Talking loud and waving your hands doesn't facilitate communication; it just makes you look weird.

Like many other aspects of life, faith has its jargon that can sometimes hinder understanding. Sanctification, justification, salvation, Advent, Communion with its symbolism of eating flesh and drinking blood – these and many other words have specific meanings to Christians that may be incomprehensible, confusing, and downright daunting to the newcomer or the seeker.

But the heart of Christianity's message centers on words that require no explanation: words such as hope, joy, love, purpose, and community. Their meanings are universal because people the world over seek them in their lives. Nobody speaks that language better than Jesus.

I didn't know if they'd even understand me [at Baylor]. They talk a lot different than Canadians.
— *Danny Watkins while he was being recruited*

Jesus speaks across all language barriers because his message of hope and meaning resounds with people everywhere.

HOW WE LEAVE

Read 2 Kings 2:1-12.

"A chariot of fire and horses of fire appeared and separated the two of them, and Elijah went up to heaven in a whirlwind" (v. 11).

Frank Bridges could win football games, but he couldn't get along with the university president, so he left.

From 1920-25, Bridges led Baylor football to a level of success it had not seen before. Two of his teams won the school's first Southwest Conference championships (1922 and '24). He left as the winningest coach in school history, and his .644 winning percentage (35-18-6) is bettered to this day only by Bob Woodruff's .645 among coaches after R.H. Hamilton, the program's first boss.

Bridges was described as "this half-pint with the tart tongue" who "came into the Southwest Conference to bewilder opponents with such shenanigans as the hidden ball trick and the kickoff from the sidelines."

His 1922 champions featured Wesley Bradshaw, a sensational back who made all-conference twice. He set a school record with 119 points, such a remarkable accomplishment that it stood until 2011 when Terrance Ganaway scored 22 touchdowns to rack up 132 points. The 1924 team went 7-2-1 overall with sophomore end/tackle/back Sam Coates among its stars.

The success of Bridges' teams on the field helped, however, to effect a dispute with Baylor's president. A report circulated in the press that Bridges had turned down two $10,000-a-year coaching jobs. The president called Bridges and told him he could never expect to make that at Baylor. "Why, I only receive $10,000," the president said. Ever quick with a quip, Bridges replied, "That's all right, Doc. I'll get you a raise."

The dispute heightened when Bridges approached the president about a raise and said he would leave if he didn't get what he wanted. Reportedly, the school leader replied, "Your resignation is accepted, Coach. Good luck and good day."

Like Frank Bridges and Elijah, we can't always choose the exact circumstances under which we leave.

You probably haven't always chosen the moves you've made in your life. Perhaps your company transferred you. A landlord didn't renew your lease. An elderly parent needed your care.

Sometimes the only choice we have about leaving is the manner in which we go, whether we depart with style and grace or not. Our exit from life is the same way. Unless we usurp God's authority over life and death, we can't choose how we die, just how we handle it. Perhaps the most frustrating aspect of dying is that we have at most very little control over the process. As with our birth, our death is in God's hands. We finally must surrender to his will even if we have spent a lifetime refusing to do so.

We do, however, control our destination. How we leave isn't up to us; where we spend eternity is — and that depends on our relationship with Jesus.

That was the first inkling I had that he didn't like me.
— Frank Bridges on his $10,000-a-year conversation with the president

How you go isn't up to you; where you go is.

A FAST START

Read Acts 2:40-47.

"Everyone was filled with awe. . . . [They] ate together with glad and sincere hearts, praising God and enjoying the favor of all the people" (vv. 43a, 46b, 47a).

It's a fact: Quincy Acy got off to the fastest start of any freshman in Big 12 history.

Acy finished his collegiate basketball career in 2012 as one of the greatest players in Baylor history. The 6-7 forward from Mesquite was part of a senior class that set school records with 100 overall wins and 35 Big 12 victories. He joined Brian Skinner as the only players in school history to finish ranked in the top 10 in scoring, rebounding, blocked shots, and field goal percentage.

Acy didn't appear to have much of a basketball future as a youngster. In the seventh and eighth grades, he couldn't even make the school's teams even though he already stood six feet tall. "I was bad," Acy admitted. But the failures motivated him, and he made the freshman team. As a sophomore, he jumped to full-time starter on the varsity squad.

Even Acy's collegiate recruiting didn't get off to a very fast start. He had to play AAU ball during the summers before any of the traditional basketball powerhouses began to take notice. One visit to Baylor clinched it for him.

Instead of passing on his senior season as so many players do, Acy returned to Waco for the 2011-12 season as the team's unquestioned leader. The Bears went 30-8 (the wins a school record) and advanced to the Elite 8 in the NCAA Tournament for the second time in three seasons. Finishing strong, Acy was named to the South Regional's All-Tournament Team.

He didn't finish quite as fast as he started, though, despite his dazzling senior season. As unlikely as it sounds, when Acy was a freshman back in 2008, he set a Big 12 record by making the first twenty shots he attempted.

Fast starts are crucial for more than basketball games and foot races. Any time we begin something new, we want to get out of the gate quickly and jump ahead of the pack and stay there. As Quincy Acy did at Baylor, we build up momentum from a fast start and keep rolling.

This is true for our faith life also. For a time after we accepted Christ as our savior, we were on fire with a zeal that wouldn't let us rest, much like the early Christians described in Acts. All too many Christians, however, let that blaze die down until only old ashes remain. We become lukewarm pew sitters.

The Christian life shouldn't be that way. Just because we were tepid yesterday doesn't mean we can't be boiling today. Every day we can turn to God for a spiritual tune-up that will put a new spark in our faith life; with a little tending that spark can soon become a raging fire. Today could be the day our faith life gets off to a fast start – again.

I loved it here as a freshman.
— *Quincy Acy on his start at Baylor*

**Every day offers us yet another chance
to get off to a fast start for Jesus.**

REVELATION

Read Isaiah 53.

"But he was pierced for our transgressions, he was
crushed for our iniquities; the punishment that brought us
peace was upon him, and by his wounds we are healed"
(v. 5).

Terrance Ganaway made a prophet out of Art Briles.

Ganaway is "arguably the most prolific running back in school history." As a senior in 2011, he was first team All-Big 12 and an honorable mention All-American as he set or tied thirteen school records. They included single-season rushing yards (1,547) and single-season rushing touchdowns (21).

Entering the 2011 season, though, Ganaway wasn't even sure if he wanted to play any more football. His time at Baylor had been disappointing. He sat out the 2008 season after transferring from Houston in the wake of his mother's death. In 2009 and 2010, he rushed for a combined total of 495 yards and left spring practice in 2011 listed behind Jarred Salubi for the starting job.

After a talk with running backs coach Jeff Lebby, though, Ganaway realized he didn't have to accept his role as a backup. He took to heart his coach's admonition that he could start if he worked hard at it. A newfound focus showed up on the field. He was indeed the starter and averaged 94 yards per game rushing through the season's first seven contests.

The Bears were only 4-3 with two straight losses heading into the Missouri game of Nov. 5. The season was on the line.

Briles spent the week pumping his running back up. Each day, the head coach repeated one message to Ganaway: "You're going to have a big night" against Missouri.

Briles' prediction came true. Ganaway rushed for 186 yards and scored two touchdowns, one of them on an 80-yard romp. The Bears defeated the Wildcats in a 42-39 thriller. They would not lose another game.

In our jaded age, we have pretty much relegated prophecy to dark rooms in which mysterious women peer into crystal balls or clasp our sweaty palms while uttering some vague generalities. At best, we understand a prophet as someone who predicts future events as Art Briles did for Terrance Ganaway.

Within the pages of the Bible, though, we encounter something radically different. A prophet is a messenger from God, one who relays divine revelation to others.

Prophets seem somewhat foreign to us because in one very real sense the age of prophecy is over. In the name of Jesus, we have access to God through our prayers and through scripture. In searching for God's will for our lives, we seek divine revelation. We may speak only for ourselves and not for the greater body of Christ, but we do not need a prophet to discern what God would have us do. What we need is faith in the one whose birth, life, and death fulfilled more than 300 Bible prophecies.

It's going to be a big week for you, G-Way. Do you feel it? You should.
— Art Briles to Terrance Ganaway before the Missouri game

Persons of faith continuously seek a word
from God for their lives.

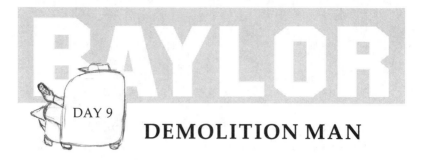

DEMOLITION MAN

Read Genesis 7.

*"Every living thing on the face of the earth was wiped
out" (v. 23a).*

Mike Singletary didn't just demolish opposing ball carriers; he
destroyed helmets.

Not many schools were too interested in looking at an under-
sized linebacker from the Houston ghettos, but Baylor assistant
coach Ron Harris was. He brought head coach Grant Teaff some
film of Singletary in action. "I honestly looked at about 10 plays
and shut the projector off," the head Bear said. "What jumped out
at me was his intensity."

So Singletary wound up in Waco in 1977 because he didn't
really have anywhere else to go. No one – not even Teaff – could
have seen at the time that a football legend was in the making.

Singletary was an All-American in 1979 and 1980. His school
records of 662 career tackles and 232 tackles in a season may
never be broken. Second on Baylor's list is linebacker Joe Pawelek,
who amassed 442 tackles from 2006-09.

Singletary's career earned him induction into both the college
and the pro halls of fame. His trademark was "the focused,
wide-eyed looks that he gave before every play." That intensity
continued with every snap as he "singlehandedly [broke] Baylor's
equipment budget by cracking 16 helmets in four years."

"The first time my helmet broke was when I hit [running back]

Dennis Gentry in practice," Singletary once recalled. "When my helmet broke, people began yelling. . . . On the next play, I hit Gentry again and my helmet split again. To get a good hit, I thought you needed to run through someone."

To prepare for Baylor's demolition man, equipment managers began keeping four or five extra helmets on hand – just in case.

We've heard a lot across recent decades about "weapons of mass destruction." The phrase conjures up frightening images of entire cities and countries being laid to waste. The population is annihilated; buildings are flattened; the infrastructure is destroyed; air and water are polluted; foodstuff is rendered inedible.

While the hideous weapons we have so zealously created can indeed wreak destruction, nothing we have can equal the weapon of mass destruction that is the wrath of God. Only once has its full fury been loosed upon his creation; the result was the mass destruction unleashed by the flood.

God has promised that he will never again destroy everything with water. When Christ returns, though, mass destruction of a particular kind will again lay waste the Earth.

Until then, as part of the ongoing battle between good and evil, we have the ultimate weapon of mass destruction at our disposal; it is our faith. With it, we play a vital part in what will be God's ultimate mass destruction: the total eradication of evil in the Day of our Lord.

I was just glad it wasn't my head.
— Mike Singletary on the first time he cracked his helmet

**Our faith is a weapon of mass destruction,
playing a key role in the eradication of evil.**

JUMPING FOR JOY

Read Luke 6:20-26.

"Rejoice in that day and leap for joy, because great is your reward in heaven" (v. 23).

Felix Obi had done enough jumping, so instead of jumping for joy, he settled for hugs to celebrate his national title.

A sophomore from El Paso, Obi entered the 2014 NCAA Indoor Track and Field Championships as the favorite in the triple jump. He had finished sixth as a freshman in 2013.

Obi was in trouble, however, before he even started, battling some knee problems that left him jumping in pain. His situation didn't improve when he fouled on his first attempt. His second try of 52 feet left him in fourth place.

Then came the biggest jump of Obi's career. He soared 54 feet 5.25 inches to break his own school record by six inches. He had set the record earlier in the year. That leap propelled him to the top of the leaderboard.

The jump also left Obi's knee done for the day. He passed on his final three attempts and could only watch everyone else try to catch him. They couldn't. "It was amazing, considering he only took three jumps," said Baylor head coach Todd Harbour.

Obi's win was the 19th NCAA indoor national title for the Baylor men's program. His win was BU's first at the indoor national meet since 2009 when Trey Harts won the 200 meters and the 4x 400-meter relay team came in first. The Baylor men continued a remarkable streak at the competition; it was the 35th straight indoor national championships at which they have scored points.

"I almost wanted to cry when I was out there," Obi said. "I just couldn't believe it, until the last jump was done."

Not willing to risk more damage to his knee, the national champion passed on jumping for joy with his teammates and coaches to celebrate the win. He did share a whole bunch of hugs.

You're probably a pretty good jumper yourself when Baylor scores against Texas. You just can't help it. It's like your feet and your seat have suddenly become magnets that repel each other. The sad part is that you always come back down to earth; the moment of exultation passes.

But what if you could jump for joy all the time? Not literally, of course; you'd pass out from exhaustion. But figuratively, with your heart aglow and joyous even when life is its most difficult.

Joy is an absolutely essential component of the Christian life. Not only do we experience joy in our public praise and worship – which is temporary – but we live daily in the joy that comes from the presence of God in our lives and the surety of his saving power extended to us through Jesus Christ.

It's not happiness, which derives from external factors; it's joy, which comes from inside.

I was competing in pain, but I knew in the end God was going to pull me through and he pulled me through with a big jump.
— Felix Obi

Unbridled joy can send you jumping all over the place; life in Jesus means such exultation is not rare but rather is a way of life.

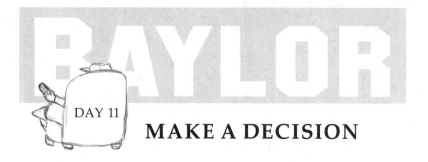

MAKE A DECISION

Read John 6:60-69.

"The words I have spoken to you are spirit and they are life. Yet there are some of you who do not believe" (vv. 63b-64a).

Robert Griffin III had already decided where he was going to play his college football — and it wasn't in Waco.

Baylor's official athletic site calls Griffin a "once-in-a-generation transcendent student-athlete [who] lifted Baylor to decades-high heights." The site says Griffin was an "exceptional athlete and leader [who] became not only [the] face of [the] Baylor football program but [an] ambassador of Baylor University [for] four years in Waco." And to think that Baylor didn't really want him and he didn't want Baylor. At least, not at first.

The coaches really started showing up during Griffin's junior season at Copperas Cove High School. They were the guys from the big-time schools, "salivating at Griffin's size and speed and saying they wanted to make the quarterback an All-America . . . defensive back or receiver." He scratched them off his list. Pedigree didn't impress him; playing quarterback did.

In the fall of 2006, Griffin visited Baylor at the urging of Bears track coach Todd Harbour, who had gamely (and unsuccessfully) tried to get Griffin to commit exclusively to track. During the trip, Griffin met Baylor head football coach Guy Morriss, who told the youngster he could play quarterback in Waco if he walked on. On the spot, Griffin decided against Baylor.

In June 2007, Griffin attended a Houston football camp and met Cougar head coach Art Briles. Impressed by Griffin's throwing ability, Briles told him he could play quarterback, so in October, he committed to Houston. In November, when Baylor fired Morriss and hired Briles, Griffin decided to follow Briles to Waco.

Thanks to that decision, Baylor athletics will never be the same again.

As with Robert Griffin III's decision to play football for Baylor, the decisions you have made along the way have shaped your life at every pivotal moment. Some decisions you made suddenly and carelessly; some you made carefully and deliberately; some were forced upon you. You may have discovered that some of those spur-of-the-moment decisions have turned out better than your carefully considered ones.

Of all your life's decisions, however, none is more important than one you cannot ignore: What have you done with Jesus? Even in his time, people chose to follow Jesus or to reject him, and nothing has changed; the decision must still be made and nobody can make it for you. Ignoring Jesus won't work either; that is, in fact, a decision, and neither he nor the consequences of your decision will go away.

Carefully considered or spontaneous – how you arrive at a decision for Jesus doesn't matter; all that matters is that you get there.

He's coming. We finally got your hurdler.
— Baylor AD Ian McCaw telling Todd Harbour of RGIII's decision

A decision for Jesus may be spontaneous or considered; what counts is that you make it.

DOWNRIGHT CRAZY

Read Luke 13:31-35.

"Some Pharisees came to Jesus and said to him, 'Leave this place and go somewhere else. Herod wants to kill you.' He replied, 'Go tell that fox . . . I must keep going today and tomorrow and the next day'" (vv. 31-33).

Since Texas was winning by seventeen points at halftime, why in the world was the Baylor quarterback smiling? Because, as he put it, "We got 'em right where we want 'em." Downright crazy. But he was right.

The Baylor-Texas game of Nov. 9, 1974, lives on in Bear lore as the "Miracle on the Brazos." The 12th-ranked Horns had beaten the Bears seventeen years in a row, and this rainy night didn't seem any different. Texas led 24-7 at halftime.

To his intense chagrin, head coach Grant Teaff spotted starting quarterback Neal Jeffrey smiling in the dressing room. "What do you see funny about being down 24-7?" he shouted. "Coach," Jeffrey replied without changing expression, "We got 'em right where we want 'em. They're thinking, 'Same old Baylor,' but we're not."

Jeffrey's downright crazy attitude spread throughout the locker room. It's exactly what the players were thinking when they took the field for the second half.

As it turned out, Jeffrey wasn't crazy at all. He was dead on.

The Bears blocked a punt and scored. Jeffrey then hit junior wide receiver Ricky Thompson with a 54-yard bomb, and suddenly it was 24-21.

When the Horns fumbled, the Bears quickly went 33 yards with senior wingback Phillip Kent -- who went on to be a church pastor -- scoring from the 6. Texas could never recover. Baylor intercepted two passes and kicked two field goals to finish off the "Miracle on the Brazos" 34-24.

"The championship was on the line," Teaff said about the game. He was just as right as Jeffrey was. The Bears went on to win the Southwest Conference title and the berth in the Cotton Bowl.

What some see as crazy often is shrewd instead. Like Neal Jeffrey's halftime attitude. Or the time you went into business for yourself or when you decided to go back to school. Maybe it was when you bought that new company's stock.

You know a good thing when you see it but are also shrewd enough to spot something that's downright crazy. Jesus was that way too. He knew that his entering Jerusalem was in complete defiance of all apparent reason and logic since a whole bunch of folks who wanted to kill him were waiting for him there.

Nevertheless, he went because he also knew that when the great drama had played out he would defeat not only his personal enemies but the most fearsome enemy of all: death itself.

It was, after all, a shrewd move that provided the way to your salvation.

We have a great game plan and we know how to come back in a game.
— Neal Jeffrey, explaining his crazy confidence at halftime of Texas '74

It's so good it sounds crazy -- but it's not: through faith in Jesus, you can have eternal life with God.

SIZE MATTERS

Read Luke 19:1-10.

"[Zacchaeus] wanted to see who Jesus was, but being a short man he could not, because of the crowd. So he ran ahead and climbed a sycamore-fig tree to see him" (vv. 3-4).

Size is overrated in all sports." So declared Lady Bears head basketball coach Kim Mulkey. Exhibit No. 1 to back up her claim is the 2013-14 season freshman forward Nina Davis put together.

Despite a senior year that earned her designation as a Parade High School All-America, Davis was overlooked by a number of colleges. "I'm sure there were schools that wrote her off in recruiting because of her size and her shot," Mulkey said.

Her size? She is 5-foot-11 and spent most of her time in high school as a guard. Her shot? A strange one "that comes almost directly from off the top of her head." Thus, many coaches saw her as too small to play forward with a shot that wouldn't let her score as a guard.

Not Mulkey. "If you can play, you can play," she asserted. So when Davis and her mom made an unofficial visit to Baylor, the head Lady Bear told the youngster she would play power forward in Waco. She would be free to roam and penetrate, but she would have to find a way to handle the bigger players who would challenge her underneath the basket. Davis was nonplussed. "It wasn't really that big of an adjustment," she remarked.

Still, when she arrived in the fall, she was the least heralded of Baylor's five-player class. She immediately demonstrated that her quickness more than compensated for her lack of size in the post. In her second college game, she scored 28 points.

Playing, as she put it, at 5-11 "with the soul of someone 6-4," Davis had a big rookie season. She was the Big 12 Freshman of the Year, first-team All-Big 12, and the conference tournament MVP. She led the conference in rebounding and was second on the Baylor squad with 15.0 points per game.

Bigger is better! Such is one of the most powerful mantras of our time. We expand our football stadiums. We augment our body parts. Hey, make that a triple cheeseburger and a large order of fries! My company is bigger than your company. Even our church buildings must be bigger to be better. About the only exception to our all-consuming drive for bigness is our waistlines.

But size obviously didn't matter to Jesus. After all, salvation came to the house of an evil tax collector who was so short he had to climb a tree to catch a glimpse of Jesus. Zacchaeus indeed had a big bank account; he was a big man in town even if his own people scorned him. But none of that – including Zacchaeus' height – mattered; Zacchaeus received salvation because of his repentance, which revealed itself in a changed life.

The same is true for us today. What matters is the size of the heart devoted to our Lord.

I might be small, but I feel like I play big.

— *Nina Davis*

**Size matters to Jesus, but only the size of the heart
of the one who would follow Him.**

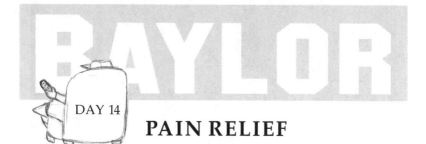

PAIN RELIEF

Read 2 Corinthians 1:3-7.

"Just as the sufferings of Christ flow over into our lives, so also through Christ our comfort overflows" (v. 5).

He was in such pain he could only hobble onto the field, but he managed to pull off the play that resulted in "the greatest upset in the first 40 years of the Southwest Conference."

Injuries kept Jack Wilson from being remembered as one of the greatest football players in Baylor history. For sure, he was one of the school's greatest natural athletes. He won the conference shot put in 1940 and '42. He was a starting guard on Bill Henderson's basketball teams of 1941 and '42. He ran the quarter mile for the track team. The starting tailback, he did it all for the football team.

"He was absolutely the best athlete I ever saw," declared guard Al Dewlen, a teammate of Wilson's. "Absolutely the Greek-God type. Beautiful muscle development."

But Wilson's luck didn't match his physique. The 1941 season illustrated the injuries that dogged him at Baylor. He suffered a ruptured kidney in the season opener. When he recovered from that, a severe ankle sprain sidelined him again.

Without their star tailback, the Bears faltered. They went into the Texas game on Nov. 8 only 3-3. The Horns were ranked No. 1 in the nation. *Life* magazine called them "the greatest team in Southwest Conference history." They were favored to whip Baylor "in a manner unfit for the eyes of sheltered women and small children." A Waco sports writer picked Texas to win 50-0 and went to College Station to watch "a good game," SMU vs. A&M.

But with 18 seconds to play, Kit Kittrell completed a 19-yard touchdown pass to Bill Coleman to make it a 7-6 game. Then, "as the afternoon shadows lengthened and the crowd grew silent," the Bears called on injured Jack Wilson to finish the miracle. He didn't limp so much as hobble onto the field, but his kick was true.

In 1956, the tie, a clear victory for the Bears, was voted the greatest upset in the conference's first forty years.

Since you live on Earth and not in Heaven, you are forced to play with pain as was Jack Wilson. Whether it's a car wreck that left you shattered, the end of a relationship that left you battered, or a loved one's death that left you tattered — pain finds you and challenges you to keep going.

While God's word teaches that you will reap what you sow, life also teaches that pain and hardship are not necessarily the result of personal failure. Pain, in fact, can be one of the tools God uses to mold your character and change your life.

What are you to do when you are hit full-speed by the awful pain that seems to choke the very will to live out of you? Where is your consolation, your comfort, and your help?

In almighty God, whose love will never fail. When life knocks you to your knees, you're closer to God than ever before.

A wounded warrior [was] given a last-second opportunity to grab a lasting taste of glory for himself and his team.
— *Writer Dave Campbell on Jack Wilson's kick vs. Texas*

When life hits you with pain, you can always turn to God for comfort, consolation, and hope.

A ROARING SUCCESS

Read Galatians 5:16-26.

*"So I say, live by the Spirit. . . . The sinful nature desires
what is contrary to the Spirit. . . . I warn you, as I did
before, that those who live like this will not inherit the
kingdom of God" (vv. 16, 17, 21).*

What Baylor's athletes accomplished in 2011-12 redefined the pinnacle of success for NCAA programs. In short, it was the most successful year in collegiate Division I athletic history.

The so-called major sports of football, men's and women's basketball, and baseball amassed 129 wins. That's the most in major college history, smashing the old record of 123 held by the University of Texas (2003-04). For one heady stretch, from Nov. 1 to Jan. 16, the football and basketball teams were a combined 40-0. Baylor's combined eighty wins (an overall 80-11 record) in those three sports were a new NCAA record.

Baylor Director of Athletics Ian McCaw said, "This was the year the unbelievable became believable at Baylor." Fittingly, he paraphrased similar remarks Robert Griffin III made during his Heisman Trophy acceptance speech in New York in December.

Three weeks after that glorious moment, the BU football team capped its 10-3 season with a win over Washington in the Alamo Bowl. In March, the men's basketball team advanced to the Elite Eight before bowing out, finishing with a 30-8 record. The women won the national title with an incredible 40-0 record; Brittany

Griner earned national player of the year honors. In the spring, the baseball team won 24 games in a row on the way to claiming the Big 12 title and advancing to an NCAA super regional.

Baylor's success, though, was much deeper and broader than just those four sports. All nineteen teams the school fielded made the postseason.

2011-12 was truly the Year of the Bear in college athletics.

Are you a successful person? Your answer, of course, depends upon how you define success. For the Bears, it's wins. But for you is the measure of your success based on the number of digits in your bank balance, the square footage of your house, that title on your office door, the size of your boat?

Certainly the world determines success by wealth, fame, prestige, awards, and possessions. Our culture screams that life is all about gratifying your own needs and wants. If it feels good, do it. It's basically the Beach Boys' philosophy of life.

But all success of this type has one glaring shortcoming: You can't take it with you. Eventually, Daddy takes the T-bird away. Like life itself, all these things are fleeting.

A more lasting way to approach success is through the spiritual rather than the physical. The goal becomes not money or backslaps by sycophants but eternal life spent with God. Success of that kind is forever.

I thought this might be a very good year for us . . ., but I never dreamed it would be like this.
— Baylor Director of Athletics Ian McCaw on the 2011-12 year

Success isn't permanent, and failure isn't fatal
— unless it's in your relationship with God.

DANCING ANGELS

Read Luke 15:1-10.

"There is rejoicing in the presence of the angels of God over one sinner who repents" (v. 10).

The quarterback cried, a safety brought out some Tostitos, fans rushed onto the field, and the league commissioner handed out a shiny new trophy. All in all, it was quite a celebration.

Four minutes into the Texas game of Dec. 7, 2013, the first heartfelt roar rippled through the Floyd Casey Stadium crowd. The public address announcer delivered the news that Oklahoma had beaten Oklahoma State. That meant the Longhorns and the Bears were now playing for the outright Big 12 championship.

What followed was a desultory first half for Baylor and a 3-3 tie at the break. "No one had to say anything at halftime because we knew the Big 12 championship was right there," said receiver Levi Norwood. "We just had to go out there and fight for it."

Which is exactly what the Bears did. On the opening possession of the last half, they marched 77 yards on 14 plays with quarterback Bryce Petty hitting receiver Antwan Goodley for an 11-yard TD to cap the drive. No one knew it at the time, but Texas was done.

By the end of the third quarter, Baylor led 20-3. Texas scored to make it 20-10, but the Bears shrugged off the touchdown and put ten straight points on the board to win going away 30-10.

The Bears were champions of the Big 12 for the first time, and the celebration began. Before the game ended, the fans chanted "B-C-S"; when the game ended, many stormed the field to join the players in celebration. Petty collapsed in tears. "I don't do that much," he said. Senior safety Ahmad Dixon showed up with two bags of Tostitos chips to celebrate a berth in the Fiesta Bowl. The Big-12 commissioner presented the championship trophy.

One thing about it: The Bears and their fans know how to celebrate a championship.

Baylor just whipped Texas. You got that new job or that promotion. You just held your newborn child in your arms. Life has those grand moments that call for celebration. You may jump up and down and scream in a wild frenzy at a Baylor game or share a quiet, sedate candlelight dinner at home — but you celebrate.

Consider then a celebration that is beyond our imagining, one that fills every niche and corner of the very home of God and the angels. Imagine a celebration in Heaven.

Those unimaginable celebrations are touched off when someone comes to faith in Jesus. Heaven itself rings with the joyous sounds of the singing and dancing of the celebrating angels. Even God rejoices when just one person – you or someone you have introduced to Christ -- turns to him.

When you said "yes" to Christ, you made the angels dance. Most importantly of all, you made God smile.

The fans who have waited a long time, I think cried more than me.
— Bryce Petty on the emotional celebration of the Big 12 title

**God himself joins the angels in heavenly
celebration when even a single person
turns to him through faith in Jesus.**

DREAM WORLD

Read Joshua 3.

"All Israel passed by until the whole nation had completed the crossing on dry ground" (v. 17b).

Whitney Canion's schoolgirl dream came true — twice.

Canion is the greatest pitcher in Baylor softball history. As a redshirt junior in 2013, she became Baylor's all-time winningest pitcher and the program's all-time strikeout leader. She was a two-time All-America and the Big 12's female Sportsperson of the Year in 2014.

In 2007, when she watched Baylor play in the Women's College World Series, she latched onto a dream: She would play for Baylor in the series. She was the Big 12 Freshman of the Year in 2009, but her dream was unrealized as the Bears lost in a super regional.

After an injury sidelined her in 2010, she returned to the field in 2011 and won 31 games, tying the school record for wins in a season set by Cristin Vitek in 2004. When the Bears beat Georgia in the super regional, Canion's dream had come true.

"To actually get a chance to play there [in Oklahoma City] is the best feeling in the world," an excited Canion declared. But Canion didn't just play there; she excelled.

The Bears' first game in the series was a nail-biter against Oklahoma State. Canion refused to give up a run, but neither did her mound opponent. The two teams traded goose eggs into the bottom of the eighth when sophomore Kelsi Kettler slammed a home run for the 1-0 win.

After a loss pushed the Bears' backs against the wall, Canion again locked up in a scoreless duel. This one, however, against Missouri, was one of the longest games in world series history. At 12:05 a.m., with two strikes and two outs in the bottom of the 13th inning, Holly Holl lined a home run to left field for the 1-0 win.

Canion's dream would be realized again when the Bears made a return trip to the world series in 2014.

No matter how tightly or how doggedly we cling to our dreams, devotion to them won't make them a reality. Moreover, the cold truth is that all too often dreams don't come true even when we put forth a mighty effort. The realization of dreams generally results from a head-on collision of persistence and timing.

But what if our dreams don't come true because they're not the same dreams God has for us? That is, they're not good enough and, in many cases, they're not big enough.

God calls us to great achievements because God's dreams for us are greater than our dreams for ourselves. Could the Israelites, wallowing in the misery of slavery, even dream of a land of their own? Could they imagine actually going to such a place?

The fulfillment of such great dreams occurs only when our dreams and God's will for our lives are the same. Our dreams should be worthy of our best – and worthy of God's involvement in making them come true.

It's crazy how dreams come true.
— Whitney Canion on playing in the Women's College World Series

**If our dreams are to come true, they must
be worthy of God's involvement in them.**

GOOD-BYE

Read John 13:33-38.

"My children, I will be with you only a little longer" (v. 33a).

After 64 seasons, the Bears in 2013 said good-bye to Floyd Casey Stadium, trading the venerable facility in for the crown jewel that is McLane Stadium on the Brazos. Once upon a time, though, the Bears' den of choice since 1950 was something to behold.

"You're dadgum right we wanted to play in the new stadium," proclaimed linebacker Gale Galloway about Baylor Stadium, which was renamed Floyd Casey Stadium in 1989. "Here was a fabulous football field with no track around it."

Galloway wasn't exaggerating; "the Baylor players had never seen anything this grand in their city." After all, they had been playing before crowds of 15,000 in wooden stands at Dutton Street's Municipal Stadium. "When the wind blew, those wooden stadiums would sway,' recalled Terry Downs, a Baylor defensive end from 1947-50. "So you better believe it was a big step going to the new stadium. The difference was night and day."

A renaissance in the Baylor football program in the late 1940s prompted the drive to build the new stadium. Only a loss to Rice in the last game of the '49 season kept the Bears from winning the Southwest Conference title. After the game, head coach Bob Woodruff told the team they would play in a new facility in 1950. "We could hardly believe it," Galloway recalled.

BEARS

Construction on the new stadium began in November 1949, but all the seats weren't in place in time for the 1950 season. That didn't slow anything down, as the facility opened on Sept. 30 with a whole lot of pomp and circumstance. And a win. Larry Isbell threw three touchdown passes and the Bears romped past Houston 34-7 before a Waco-record 24,500 fans.

Now that field is history. While Floyd Casey Stadium held many fond memories, saying good-bye to it wasn't nearly as painful as watching someone you love drive off. Maybe it was a child leaving home for the first time or your best friend moving halfway across the country. It's an extended – maybe even per-manent – separation, and good-byes hurt.

Jesus felt the pain of parting too. Throughout his brief ministry, Jesus had been surrounded by and had depended upon his friends and confidants, the disciples. About to leave them, he gathered them for a going-away supper and gave them a heads-up about what was about to happen. In the process, he offered them words of comfort. What a wonderful friend he was! Even though he was the one who was about to suffer unimaginable agony, Jesus' concern was for the pain his friends would feel.

But Jesus wasn't just saying good-bye. He was on his mission of providing the way through which none of us would ever have to say good-bye again.

It was magnificent. It was an honor to play there, but the new stadium is going to be awesome.
— Halfback Don Carpenter (1950-52) on the two Baylor stadiums

**Through Jesus, we will see the day
when we say good-bye to good-byes.**

USING YOUR HEAD

Read Job 28.

"The fear of the Lord -- that is wisdom, and to shun evil is understanding" (v. 28).

Art Briles had to say exactly the right thing to keep a star lineman in Waco. So he thought his words out carefully, especially the part about Cadillacs and horse ranches.

As he had known since his days of coaching high-school players, Briles understood that a football team's success always begins up front. Any offensive lineman with NFL potential was thus a key to winning games. Baylor had such a player on hand when Briles took over the program in November 2007.

He was tackle Jason Smith, a rising senior. The problem lay in the fact that Smith was frustrated and ready to turn pro after being part of only twelve wins in three seasons. Briles crafted a plan to keep Smith on campus. He asked around and found out some things about his unsettled star lineman, including the facts that he was big into horses and ranching and loved his grandmother.

When Smith approached him in the weight room, Briles was ready. He told Smith that if he left Baylor, he would be drafted, probably in the middle rounds. "But you're only going to make so much money," he said. Then he delivered his carefully thought-out punch line. "If you stay, I'll guarantee you this: there's a big difference between visiting the ranch and owning the ranch."

That grabbed Smith's attention, and Briles followed up with his clincher. "You can either buy your grandma a car or a Cadillac," he said.

The logic was inescapable, as was the fact that his coach had cared enough to learn something about him. Smith stayed and was All-America in 2008. He was drafted No. 2 overall and signed a $33 million contract. His first two purchases were a Cadillac for his grandmother and a 1,000-acre horse ranch for himself.

You're a thinking person. When you talk about using your head, you're speaking as Art Briles illustrated in his talk with Jason Smith: Logic and reason are part of your psyche. A coach's bad call frustrates you and your children's inexplicable behavior flummoxes you. Why can't people just think things through?

That goes for matters of faith too. Jesus doesn't tell you to turn your brain off when you walk into a church or open the Bible. In fact, when you seek Jesus, you seek him heart, soul, body, and mind. The mind of the master should be the master of your mind so that you consider every situation in your life through the critical lens of the mind of Christ. With your head and your heart, you encounter God, who is, after all, the true source of wisdom.

To know Jesus is not to stop thinking; it is to start thinking divinely.

We didn't worry about the draft. We just focused on the season and let everything take care of itself.
— Jason Smith on Art Briles' plan for him and the 2008 football season

Since God is the source of all wisdom,
it's only logical that you encounter him
with your mind as well as your emotions.

DAY 20

UNBELIEVABLE!

Read Hebrews 3:7-19.

"See to it, brothers, that none of you has a sinful, unbelieving heart that turns away from the living God" (v. 12).

What the Bears did against Kansas was simply unbelievable.

On Nov. 12, 2011, Baylor rolled over and died for three quarters, trailing the Jayhawks 24-3 heading into the final period. Winless in the big 12, Kansas had held Robert Griffin III and the explosive Bear offense to just 190 yards.

Griffin created the first real excitement of the day when he broke loose down the left sideline for a 49-yard touchdown run with 11:45 to play. The Bears still trailed by 14 big points, and the situation didn't appear to improve much after a Kansas punt left the boys from Waco sitting at their own 2-yard line.

But the suddenly inspired Bears drove 98 yards, finishing off the drive with a 36-yard pass from Griffin to Terrance Williams. With 7:58 on the clock, a comeback didn't seem so impossible now.

The defense rose up, getting the ball back to Griffin and his cohorts at their own 20 with 4:07 to play. Griffin then tossed what he called "the best worst pass I ever threw in my life." It was "a wounded duck that seemed to flutter in the wind forever." Tevin Reese hauled in that wounded duck and turned it into a 67-yard touchdown that tied the game at 24 with 3:32 remaining.

The game went into overtime, and the Bears kept their momentum when Griffin found Reese again for a 14-yard score. Aaron Jones kicked the PAT for Baylor's first lead of the game.

Kansas responded with a touchdown of its own and then went for the win with the two-point conversion try. When cornerback Joe Williams batted the pass away, Baylor had 31-30 win.

"It was the biggest comeback [I've] ever been a part of," said a dazed Griffin right after the game. It was also the biggest fourth-quarter comeback in Baylor history — and the most unbelievable.

Much of what taxes the limits of our belief system has little effect on our lives. Maybe we don't believe in UFOs, honest politicians, aluminum baseball bats, Sasquatch, or the viability of electric cars. A healthy dose of skepticism is a natural defense mechanism that helps protect us in a world that all too often has designs on taking advantage of us.

That's not the case, however, when Jesus and God are part of the mix. Quite unbelievably, we often hear people blithely assert they don't believe in God. Or brazenly declare they believe in God but don't believe Jesus was anything but a good man and a great teacher.

At this point, unbelief becomes dangerous because God doesn't fool around with scoffers. He locks them out of the Promised Land, which isn't a country in the Middle East but Heaven itself.

Given that scenario, it's downright unbelievable that anyone would not believe.

I can't quite believe what I saw that afternoon.
— Sportswriter John Werner on Baylor's 2011 win over Kansas

Perhaps nothing is as unbelievable as that some people insist on not believing in God or his son.

CHOICES

Read Deuteronomy 30:15-20.

"I have set before you life and death, blessings and curses.
Now choose life, so that you and your children may live"
(v. 19).

Two choices determined Chris McAllister's college football career, one he made and one that was made for him.

Five days before Christmas in 2008, McAllister chose Baylor as the school where he would play his college ball. Some of his buddies "shook their heads and wondered if he'd lost his mind." After all, McAllister had some big-time, winning programs making him offers. Baylor was into its second decade without a bowl.

"I trusted in Coach Briles," McAllister explained. The head coach convinced him Baylor was about to turn the corner. "Baylor gave me a different level of comfort than other schools."

McAllister redshirted in 2009 and was a starter at middle linebacker by the end of the 2010 season. Everything changed, however, when Phil Bennett became Baylor's defensive coordinator in January 2011.

"I walked into his office and sat down, and he told me he was moving me to defensive end before he introduced himself," McAllister recalled. He had no choice, no voice in the decision. "He was like 'Who is this guy?'" Bennett remembered.

McAllister had not played defensive end since his sophomore year of high school and never thought he'd go back there in college. He didn't want to make the move despite Bennett's insistence. He went along with it for the good of the team.

Progress was slow at first. "I was a little out of shape and a step behind," McAllister admitted. But in the spring of 2012, he began to get the hang of it and was a starter his last two seasons, blossoming into a star. He was twice All-Big 12 First Team and was the defensive MVP of the 2012 Holiday Bowl.

That choice was a good one, as was his choice of a school. He played on four bowl teams and a Big 12 champion.

As with Chris McAllister, your life is the sum of the choices you've made. That is, you have arrived at this moment and this place in your life because of the choices you made in your past. Your love of the Bears. Your spouse or the absence of one. Mechanic, teacher, or beautician. Condo in downtown Dallas or ranch home in Waco. Dog, cat, or goldfish. You chose; you live with the results.

That includes the most important choice you will ever have to make: faith or the lack of it. That we have the ability to make decisions when faced with alternatives is a gift from God, who allows that faculty even when he's part of the choice. We can choose whether or not we will love him. God does remind us that this particular choice has rather extreme consequences: Choosing God's way is life; choosing against him is death.

Life or death. What choice is that?

When I chose Baylor, my friends were making fun of me.
— Chris McAllister

God gives you the freedom to choose: life or death;
what kind of choice is that?

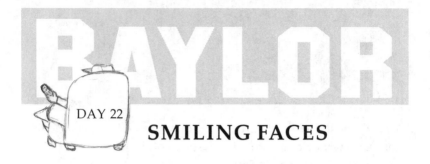

SMILING FACES

Read Isaiah 35.

"[E]verlasting joy will crown their heads. Gladness and joy will overtake them" (v. 10).

Nichole Jones often smiled at those she met at the starting line — right before she left them in the dust.

Jones is one of the greatest runners in Baylor history. From 2006-10, she garnered a number of All-American honors while setting several school records. She still holds the Baylor record for the 1,000 meters outdoor and 800 meters indoor.

Jones stood only 5'2" tall, but she was called "a quiet giant, both athletically and spiritually, who'd rather show you what she's about than tell you." What she showed while she was in Waco was her speed and her faith — and her smile.

Early on, Jones realized she had some athletic skills. Exactly how to use them, however, was another matter. She was cut from her middle school volleyball team. After she made her school's basketball team, her coach instructed her not to move on the court so she wouldn't mess up. In the summer before her seventh grade, Jones defaulted to running because, as she put it, "running doesn't require a lot of coordination."

Even the running didn't start out well. She ran a two-mile race one time and was lapped twice. She kept on practicing, and the next year she was lapped only once. A year later, she kept pace with the pack.

With quiet confidence, Jones kept on getting better. That confidence, though, was rooted in her faith in Christ, not faith in her God-given talent. "The whole process was a complete step of faith," she once said. "I'm running to be a witness for God."

The joy she found in her faith showed in her running. That's where the smile came in. She wore it while she left her competitors behind, so much so that Todd Harbour, Baylor's head track/cross country coach, dubbed her "The Smiling Assassin."

What does your smile say about you? What is it that makes you smile and laugh in the first place? Your dad's corny jokes? Your children or grandchildren? A Baylor touchdown?

When you smile, the ones who love you and whom you love can't help but return the favor — and the joy. It's like turning on a bright light in a world threatened by darkness.

Besides, you have good reason to walk around all the time with a smile on your face not because of something you have done but rather because of what God has done for you. As a result of his great love for you, God acted through Jesus to give you free and eternal salvation. That should certainly make you smile as it did Nicole Jones when she ran.

But there's more. Jesus isn't through with this fallen world. One day he will return, and Heaven on Earth will become a reality. We'll be right there with him to share it all.

Basking in his glory, we'll be smiling the whole time.

She'll smile at you and then just beat you bad.
— *Todd Harbour on Nichole Jones*

It's so overused it's become a cliché, but it's true nevertheless: Smile! God loves you.

DRY RUN

Read John 4:1-15.

*"Everyone who drinks this water will be thirsty again,
but whoever drinks the water I give him will never thirst.
Indeed, the water I give him will become in him a spring
of water welling up to eternal life" (vv. 13-14).*

The drought was of biblical proportions; it lasted sixteen years. When the time came for it to end, even the weather conspired to stretch it out.

Baylor's football team of 2010 had a clear goal in mind: get to a bowl game. With 35 postseason contests on the NCAA schedule, that didn't sound like much, but the Bears had not played in a bowl game since the Alamo Bowl of 1994.

Robert Griffin III had recovered from the knee injury that had sidelined him for most of the '09 season, so the squad appeared to have the pieces in place to make a serious run at a bowl game. And so it did.

Easy wins over Sam Houston State and Buffalo launched the campaign. After a thumping from TCU, the Bears rallied to beat Rice and Kansas handily. Texas Tech won by seven points for the third straight season, but the team bounced back again with a big 31-25 defeat of Colorado.

That left the Bears sitting at 5-2 with Kansas State coming to town on Oct. 23. The two squads played a wild one. Tailback Jay Finley set a school record with 250 yards rushing, and Griffin achieved a personal milestone with 404 yards passing. The Bears needed every yard to pull out a 47-42 win in what was called "the biggest win for the program in more than a decade."

That's because the win was the Bears' sixth of the season, and they were bowl eligible, eventually landing in the Texas Bowl. To win, the Bears had to battle both the Wildcats and the weather as lightning forced a 107-minute delay. "Man, it really is that hard to be bowl eligible at Baylor," head coach Art Briles quipped.

He could joke all he wanted to. The drought was over.

You can walk across that river you boated on in the spring. The city's put all neighborhoods on water restriction. That beautiful lawn you fertilized and seeded will turn a sickly, pale green and may lapse all the way to brown. Somebody wrote "Wash Me" on the rear window of your truck.

The sun bakes everything, including the concrete. The earth itself seems exhausted, just barely hanging on. It's a drought.

It's the way a soul that shuts God out looks.

God instilled the physical sensation of thirst in us to warn us of our body's need for water. He also gave us a spiritual thirst that can be quenched only by his presence in our lives. Without God, we are like tumbleweeds, dried out and windblown, offering the illusion of life where there is only death.

Living water – the water of life – is readily available in Jesus. We may drink our fill, and thus we slake our thirst and end our soul's drought – forever.

That was the day Baylor football finally got over the proverbial hump.
— Nick Eatman on the drought-ending win over K-State

Our soul thirsts for God's refreshing presence.

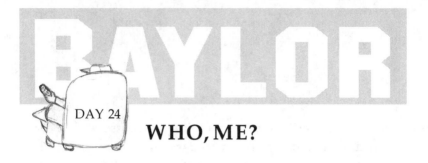

WHO, ME?

Read Judges 6:11-23.

"'But Lord,' Gideon asked, 'how can I save Israel? My clan is the weakest in Manasseh, and I am the least in my family'" (v. 15).

KD Cannon was just minding his own business, not expecting to play anytime soon. Seconds later, he was scoring a touchdown.

Cannon was an All-American wide receiver in high school, but he expected to spend his 2014 freshman season gradually working his way onto the field at Baylor. After all, the Bears had Antwan Goodley, Clay Fuller, and Levi Norwood for senior quarterback Bryce Petty to throw to.

The 2014 season opener was a special one, the first game ever played at brand spanking new McLane Stadium. The occasion marked the first football game to be played on campus since 1935. A statue of Heisman-Trophy winner Robert Griffin III was dedicated, and he took part in the ceremonies. He also was on the field to deliver the invocation and take part in the coin toss.

The opposition for the day came from SMU, which was overmatched from the outset as the game quickly got out of hand. (Baylor won 45-0.) The Mustangs fumbled right off the bat to set up a 4-yard scoring run from Shock Linwood. Three plays later, Linwood's 45-yard punt return preceded Petty's 3-yard touchdown pass to tight end Tre'Von Armstead.

Cannon was an interested observer during all this with little thought of getting into the action. Thus, he was caught off guard when head coach Art Briles bellowed out his name. "What?" he responded. "Get in," Briles ordered.

That was surprising enough, but then Petty called Cannon's number in the huddle. The rookie broke open by blowing past the SMU defense, and Petty obliged with a strike. Cannon turned the completion into a 46-yard touchdown on his first play and first catch in a Baylor uniform.

You've experienced a "Who-me?" moment in your life, and it probably wasn't as much fun as KD Cannon's was. How about that time the teacher called on you when you hadn't done a lick of homework? Or the night the hypnotist pulled you out of a room full of folks to be his guinea pig? You've had the wide-eyed look and the turmoil in your midsection when you were suddenly singled out and found yourself in a situation you neither sought nor were prepared for.

You may feel exactly as Gideon did about being called to serve God in some way, quailing at the very notion of being audacious enough to teach Sunday school, coordinate a high school prayer club, or lead a small group study. Who, me? Hey, who's worthy enough to do anything like that?

The truth is that nobody is — but that doesn't seem to matter to God. And it's his opinion, not yours, that counts.

I wasn't expecting to get the ball, but [Bryce Petty] was like, 'High-low go.' I was like, 'That's me!'
— KD Cannon's who-me moment during his first play on the field

**You're right in that no one is worthy to serve God,
but the problem is that doesn't matter to God.**

PRAYER WARRIORS

Read Luke 18:1-8.

"Then Jesus told his disciples a parable to show them that they should always pray and not give up" (v. 1).

Doctors gave Mariah Chandler up for dead. Then her mother prayed.

A graduate student in 2013-14, Chandler wrapped up her Baylor career as a part-time starter at forward who saw action in 26 games during Baylor's run to 32 wins and the Sweet Sixteen. She played each game and lived every day with a perspective unusual for one so young. She was keenly and honestly thankful for each day and for the aspects of her life most young people take for granted: family, friends, teammates, an education.

That's because when she was 7 years old, she died.

"It was a typical day," Chandler remembered. "We were just swimming. I started coughing really, really bad." It wouldn't go away. Doctors diagnosed her with a rare heart disorder, and she went in for surgery. Complications arose, and the surgical team couldn't revive her. "The doctors called it; she was gone."

After Mariah's mother, Alicia, received the awful news, she walked into the room to view her daughter's body. But she did much more than that: She cried out to God for a miracle, begging and pleading with God not to take her daughter. God heard the mother's prayer of desperation and love, and he answered it.

As Mariah told it, Alicia "was crying, like a typical mother, really hysterical." And in between her crying and her praying, Alicia suddenly heard the beeping of Mariah's heart monitor.

Flabbergasted doctors admitted no medical explanation could be offered for Mariah Chandler's recovery. The only answer was the true one: God had answered a distraught, faithful mother's prayer. It was a miracle, a nickname Mariah still carries.

Alicia Chandler prayed and didn't give up. That's what Jesus taught us to do as his followers: always pray and never give up.

Any problems we may have with prayer and its results derive from our side, not God's. We pray for a while about something – perhaps fervently at first – but our enthusiasm wanes if we don't receive the answer we want exactly when we want it. Why waste our time by asking for the same thing over and over again?

But God isn't deaf; God does hear our prayers, and God does respond to them. As Jesus clearly taught, our prayers have an impact because they turn the power of Almighty God loose in this world. Thus, falling to our knees and praying to God is not a sign of weakness and helplessness. Rather, praying for someone or something is an aggressive act, an intentional ministry, a conscious and fervent attempt on our part to change someone's life or the world for the better.

God responds to our prayers; we often just can't perceive or don't understand how he is working to make those prayers come about.

She prayed over me. She was just praying, 'God, I don't want you to take my baby. Whatever you need to do, just bring her back.'
    — Mariah Chandler on her mother's prayers at her bedside

Jesus taught us to always pray and never give up.

GOOD ADVICE

Read Isaiah 8:11-9:7.

"And he will be called Wonderful Counselor" (v. 9:6b).

Art Briles had some advice for Nick Florence, but it sure wasn't anything the quarterback was expecting.

In the spring of 2012, reality set in at Baylor: RGIII and the exciting ride he brought with him were over and done with. Nick Florence was the heir apparent. "I just had this good feeling about him," Briles would say late in spring practice that year. "He's got that instinct as a leader and just understands how to get people to go with him."

That confidence in Florence didn't mean, however, Briles had no advice for the successor to the most storied quarterback in school history. Shortly before two-a-day practices began in the summer, the head Bear summoned Florence to the weight room.

The coach told his next starting quarterback that the general perception of him was as "this pretty boy who's perfect and doesn't make mistakes. You need to dirty it up." Briles advised Florence to let his beard and his hair grow out.

The somewhat perplexed senior wasn't convinced Briles was serious until the coach sent him a text later that evening. It had a picture of Snoop Dogg and Martha Stewart cooking in a kitchen with a caption that said, "One of these is a convicted felon." Briles added, "Obviously, it's not the one everyone thinks it'll be."

Florence got the message, avoiding all clippers and scissors for several months. Whether the shaggy look affected the way his teammates played for him is questionable, but the hirsute senior was unquestionably the leader of the 2012 squad as he set or tied eight school records.

Like Nick Florence, we all need a little advice now and then. More often than not, we turn to professional counselors, who are all over the place. Marriage counselors, grief counselors, guidance counselors in our schools, rehabilitation counselors, all sorts of mental health and addiction counselors — we even have pet counselors. No matter what our situation or problem, we can find plenty of advice for the taking.

The problem, of course, is that we find advice easy to offer but hard to swallow. We also have a rueful tendency to solicit the wrong source for advice, seeking counsel that doesn't really solve our problem but that instead enables us to continue with it.

Our need for outside advice, for an independent perspective on our situation, is actually God-given. God serves many functions in our lives, but one role clearly delineated in his Word is that of Counselor. Jesus himself is described as the "Wonderful Counselor." All the advice we need in our lives is right there for the asking; we don't even have to pay for it except with our faith. God is always there for us: to listen, to lead, and to guide.

You're not going to be like Samson, are you? He cut his hair and he lost his power.
— Art Briles when he noticed Nick Florence had trimmed his bangs

We all need and seek advice in our lives,
but the ultimate and most wonderful counselor
is of divine and not human origin.

PLEASE!

Read Matthew 7:7-11.

"Ask and it will be given you; seek and you will find; knock and the door will be opened for you" (v. 7).

Kim Mulkey wanted to stay home so badly that she got down on her knees and begged. Then she went to Waco.

Mulkey has been called "the undisputed queen of women's basketball in Texas." Since she took over the Baylor program in 2000, the Lady Bears have never won fewer than 21 games and have missed the NCAA Tournament only once. Her record at Baylor through the 2014-15 season was 437-90 and, of course, the program has two national titles.

While Mulkey is now synonymous with women's basketball in Waco, back in 2000 she didn't want to leave Ruston, La., even when Baylor made an offer. A Louisiana native, she had devoted 19 years of her life — four as a player and 15 as an assistant coach — to the La. Tech program. Ruston and La. Tech were home for her.

Legendary Tech head coach Leon Barmore stepped aside at age 55 "to make way for his hand-picked successor." The school offered Mulkey the job, but there was a very big catch. Mulkey believed that she needed five years to make the program hers. A five-year contract was standard procedure for up-and-coming coaches, she argued. She certainly classified, having turned down several head coaching offers from big-time programs. Tech, however, offered only a four-year contract.

Desperate to stay in Ruston but not willing to compromise on her contract, Mulkey begged for her professional life. In the office of the school president, she dropped to her knees and pleaded with him for the five-year contract, tears running down her face.

When she realized what she was doing — that she had sunk as low as she could go — she wiped her face, stood up, and marched out of the office to a phone. She called Baylor and accepted the school's job offer. "Sometimes you thank God for unanswered prayers," she said years later.

Whether it's for the one you love to marry you, for a raise, for justice in traffic court, you'll ask for what you want, but you won't beg. Western society still stigmatizes begging. You may hand some money to the person holding a pleading sign along the road, but you probably also wonder why that beggar doesn't get a job.

As it was with Kim Mulkey at Louisiana Tech, begging is born of desperation, when it's all you have left and you're stripped of any sense of shame or pride. Inherent in such a situation is an imbalance of power; the one doing the begging has none.

Such is obviously the case in our relationship with God. We have no power, and we don't call God "almighty" for nothing. God has unimaginable power at his command. Fortunately, he chooses to temper that power with his love.

God doesn't want us coming to him as a last resort, when we have nowhere else to turn. God asks only that we ask — not beg.

The word for what I did in that office is 'grovel.' That's how badly I didn't want to leave home. Man, how low did I go?
— Kim Mulkey on begging the La. Tech president for a contract

God doesn't require that we beg, only that we ask.

FOR THE FUN OF IT

Read Nehemiah 8:1-12.

"Do not grieve, for the joy of the Lord is your strength"
(v. 10c).

As head coaches do, Baylor's John Bridgers drew a whole bunch of criticism for the way he approached football. Among his problems with his detractors? He made football too much fun.

Bridgers was the head Bear from 1959-68, compiling a record of 49-53-1. Three of his teams went to bowl games and won two of them.

During the 4-6 season of 1962, the alums went after Bridgers' job. They charged him with being too soft on his players and of keeping on the squad players who weren't good enough. Bridgers unashamedly pled guilty to those and other "heretical practices which, should they become accepted, might unravel the woof and warp of heavy-pressure college football."

Bridgers indeed never cut a player from a Baylor squad just because he wasn't good enough. He never eased a player out of college to save a scholarship for a better player. He never shouted at his players or criticized them openly in practice, a time when laughter was considered as much a part of the day as calisthenics.

Bridgers refused to bench his players when they made mistakes. "They're college boys," he said, "not paid professionals." A man of unbending principle, he believed the violation of a rule drew the same penalty for the team's star as for a bench-warmer.

Another "shortcoming" Bridgers had was that even the faculty liked him. "He's changed my ideas about football not belonging on the college campus," said one history professor.

For John Bridgers, football was first and foremost supposed to be fun.

A very erroneous stereotype of the Christian lifestyle has emerged, that of a dour, sour-faced person always on the prowl to sniff out fun and frivolity and shut it down. "Somewhere, sometime, somebody's having fun – and it's got to stop!" Many understand this to be the mandate that governs the Christian life.

But even the Puritans, from whom that American stereotype largely comes, had parties, wore bright colors, and allowed their children to play games.

God's attitude toward fun is clearly illustrated by Nehemiah's instructions to the Israelites after Ezra had read them God's commandments. They broke out into tears because they had failed God, but Nehemiah told them not to cry but to eat, drink, and be merry instead. Go have fun, believers! Celebrate God's goodness and forgiveness!

This is still our mandate today because a life spent in an awareness of God's presence is all about celebrating, rejoicing, and enjoying God's countless gifts, especially salvation in Jesus Christ. To live for Jesus is to truly know the fun in living.

John Dixon Bridgers is a refreshing iconoclast who not only believes that football is a game but thinks it should be played for fun.
— Sports Illustrated *writer Morton Shamik*

What on God's wonderful Earth can be more fun than living for Jesus.

DAY 29

UNCERTAIN TIMES

Read Psalm 18:1-6, 20-29.

"The Lord is my rock . . . in whom I take refuge. He is my shield, and the horn of my salvation, my stronghold" (v. 2).

You would think the outcome of a college football game would be one of life's certainties. But then there's the Baylor-TCU game of 1907.

Baylor's first-ever football season (1899) included a 0-0 tie with the Horned Frogs. The school was then known as AddRan College after its founders; its name was not changed officially to Texas Christian University until 1902. It was also in Waco at the time, which made for an immediate rivalry. The school moved to Ft. Worth in 1910 after the main building in Waco burned.

The schools played each other more than once in those early years. After not meeting in 1900, they played twice in 1901 with Baylor romping to a pair of wins. In 1902 and then from 1904-09 (except for 1906 when Baylor didn't field a team), the schools met three times each season. The logic behind the frequent meetings probably had something to do with not having to travel. In 1911, after TCU left Waco, the schools switched to an annual game.

The first meeting of the 1907 season, which would see Baylor go 4-3-1, was a 6-6 tie. The second encounter, however, left the players and the fans uncertain about who really won.

The TCU record book shows an 11-10 win for the Frogs. For

many years, however, the Baylor record book listed the game as a 10-9 win for the Bears.

The uncertainty arose because of a controversial call regarding a safety late in the game. The officials disagreed about whether a Baylor ball carrier was actually tackled in his own end zone. The problem lay in the goal line, which had disappeared amid all the dust and dirt. While the officials debated the matter, the players and the spectators simply "went home to supper with their own convictions about the final score."

Even when we believe Baylor will field another great football team, we have some uncertainty because nothing in sport is a sure thing. If it were, it wouldn't be any fun.

Life is like that. We never know what's in store for us or what's going to happen next. We can be riding high one day with a job promotion, good health, a nice family, and sunny weather. Only a short time later, we can be unemployed, sick, divorced, and/or broke. When we place our trust in life itself and its rewards, we are certain to face uncertain times.

We must search out a haven, a place where we know we can find certainty to ease our trepidation and anxiety about life's uncertainties. We can find that haven, that rock, by dropping to our knees. There, we can find that certainty – every time.

Our life and times are uncertain. The Lord God Almighty is sure – and is only a prayer away.

Only recently have both institutions agreed to record the [1907] game as an 11-10 win for TCU.
                                        — *Writer Alan J. Lefever in 2013*

Only God offers certainty amid life's uncertainty.

THE BIG TIME

Read Revelation 21:22-27; 22:1-6.

"They will see his face, and his name will be on their foreheads. . . . And they will reign for ever and ever" (vv. 22:4, 5c).

There is little doubt exactly when the Baylor Bears finished off their climb back into the big time of college football: Nov. 19, 2011.

On that night, in Floyd Casey Stadium, Robert Griffin III hit Terrance Williams with a 34-yard touchdown pass with 8 seconds left in the game. The score gave the 25th-ranked Bears a stunning 45-38 win over the fifth-ranked Oklahoma Sooners.

On that night, the Bears "wiped out all those Oklahoma ghosts that had taken up residence" wherever the two teams played. On that night, the most frustrating streak in Baylor football history came to a sudden and dramatic end.

In a series that began in 1901, the Bears had gone 0-20 against Oklahoma with fifteen of the defeats coming in Big 12 play. The win was exhilarating, but breaking the streak in itself wasn't significant enough to propel the Baylor program back into the ranks of big-time college football. It's that the Sooners were ranked so high, that they still had their eyes on a national title.

"We were looking for a signature win, and we finally got it," Griffin explained.

The Sooners had apparently sent the game into overtime by scoring with 51 seconds to forge a tie. Baylor got the ball at its own 20 with no time outs left — but it had its Heisman-Trophy winner. Griffin scrambled twice for yardage and then hit Kendall Wright for 12 yards to the Sooner 34. He then rolled to his left and fired a bullet to Williams across the field for the game winner.

Baylor's quarterback didn't see the catch. "I got hit and was on the ground," Griffin said. "Then one of our offensive linemen picked me up and said we just won the game."

They had indeed. They had also made one big leap back into the big time.

As those associated with Baylor football did for a while, we often look around at our current situation and dream of hitting the big time. We might look longingly at that vice-president's office or daydream about the day when we're the boss, maybe even of our own business. We may scheme about ways to make a lot of money, or at least more than we're making now. We may even consciously seek out fame and power.

Making it big is just part of the American dream. It's the heart of that which drives immigrants to leave everything they know and come to this country.

The truth, though, is that all of this so-called "big-time" stuff we so earnestly cherish is actually only small potatoes. If we want to speak of what is the real big-time, we better think about God and his dwelling place in Heaven. There we not only see God and Jesus face to face, but we reign. God puts us in charge.

For me personally, that was the moment this program changed.
— Quarterback Bryce Petty on the win over OU

**Living with God, hanging out with Jesus,
and reigning in Heaven – now that's big time.**

THE FAME GAME

Read 1 Kings 10:1-10, 18-29.

"King Solomon was greater in riches and wisdom than all the other kings of the earth. The whole world sought audience with Solomon" (vv. 23-24).

Already famous at Baylor, Darryl Middleton had big dreams of fame and fortune playing pro basketball. He just didn't realize he would have to travel halfway around the world to achieve them.

Middleton was a star at Baylor from 1985-88. A 6-7 forward, he was twice first-team All-Southwest Conference. He was inducted into the Baylor Athletic Hall of Fame in 2010 and was named to Baylor's 17-member All-Centennial team in 2006. Middleton still ranks among the Bears' career leaders in points, rebounds, and field-goal percentage.

Fame and fortune beckoned when Middleton was drafted in 1988 by the Atlanta Hawks, but he couldn't crack what was then a pretty loaded roster. When a coach asked him if he was interested in playing in Turkey, Middleton didn't know they played basketball there. Soon, though, his wife and he headed overseas

That was in 1988. He was named the league's MVP that first season, and he returned to America hoping to catch onto an NBA team. He didn't, so he went back to Europe — this time to Milan.

In essence, Middleton never came home again. Over the next 25 years, he couldn't find work in the states, but any number of European teams were always eager to sign him. He changed clubs 15 times in five countries and was consistently one of the best players, three times the MVP of the Spanish league. From Spain to Russia, he played for ten championship teams.

And he kept playing, right on up until 2014 when he was 47. Middleton was so good for so long that he became one of the most famous and most respected of Europe's American players.

Have you ever wanted to be famous? Hanging out with other rich and famous people, having folks with microphones listen to what you say, throwing money around like toilet paper, meeting adoring and clamoring fans, signing autographs, and posing for the paparazzi before you climb into your imported sports car?

Many of us yearn to be famous, well-known in the places and by the people that we believe matter. That's all fame amounts to: strangers knowing your name and your face.

The truth is that you are already famous where it really does matter, which excludes TV's talking heads, screaming teenagers, rapt moviegoers, or D.C. power brokers. You are famous because Almighty God knows your name, your face, and everything else there is to know about you.

If a persistent photographer snapped you pondering this fame – the only kind that has eternal significance – would the picture show the world unbridled joy or the shell-shocked expression of a mug shot?

Darryl Middleton is by all accounts one of the most famous American players in European basketball history.
> — *Sam Borden of the* New York Times

**You're already famous because
God knows your name and your face.**

GOOD NEWS

Read Matthew 28:1-10.

'"He has risen from the dead and is going ahead of you into Galilee. There you will see him.' Now I have told you" (v. 7).

O n Nov. 17, 2012, college football was abuzz across the entire country with one piece of gigantic, shocking news: The Baylor Bears had pummeled the Kansas State Wildcats.

Why was this such a big deal? After all, Baylor had beaten K-State twice before in the fledgling Big-12 rivalry. Well, there's this for starters: the Wildcats went into the game 10-0, ranked No. 1 and rolling toward the national championship game. The Bears, on the other hand, were a mere 4-5 and were battling for any kind of bowl game.

There's more. K-State was averaging nearly 50 points per game; the Bears were last in the country in total defense. Moreover, Baylor was 0-11-1 all time against top-ranked teams.

So, it was a fluke, right? The Bears got lucky with some bounces and a last-gasp Hail-Mary pass that deflected off two defenders. No, not at all, and that was as newsworthy as the outcome itself. As sportswriter Will Parchman said, this was "not some fly-by-night upset. This was a dismantling of the highest order." The Bears simply ran the Cats right out of Floyd Casey Stadium.

Nick Florence passed for 238 yards, Lache Seastrunk ran for a career-high 185 yards, and Glasco Martin rushed for another 113 (and scored three touchdowns). The defense intercepted K-State's Heisman-Trophy candidate of a quarterback three times. Overall, Baylor had a 580-362 edge in total offense.

"All week we believed we were going to beat them" Florence said. "We didn't want to be surprised when it happened." The Bears may have been the only ones not surprised by the news.

Oh, yes, the score. A humiliating 52-24, which was as newsworthy as the upset itself.

The story of mankind's "progress" through the millennia could be summarized and illustrated quite well in an account of how we disseminate our news. For much of recorded history, we told our stories through word of mouth, which required time to spread across political and geographical boundaries. That method also didn't do much to ensure accuracy.

Today, though, our news — like Baylor's upset of Kansas State — is instantaneous. Yesterday's news is old news; we want to see it and hear about it as it happens.

But the biggest news story in the history of the world goes virtually unnoticed every day by the so-called mainstream media. It is, in fact, often treated as nothing more than superstition. But it's true, and it is the greatest, most wonderful news of all.

What headline should be blaring from every news source in the world? This one: "Jesus Rises from Dead, Defeats Death." It's still today's news, and it's still the most important news story ever.

We beat the socks off these guys.
— Baylor's Ahmad Dixon on the big news that Baylor beat K-State

**The biggest news story in history took place
when Jesus Christ walked out of that tomb.**

WHO'S THE BOSS?

Read Matthew 28:16-20.

"Then Jesus came to them and said, 'All authority in heaven and on earth has been given to me'" (v. 18).

Veteran head coach Steve Smith is clearly the boss of the Baylor baseball team. Once, though, one of his pitchers told him what to do — and he did it.

The 2015 season marked Smith's 21st at the helm of the Baylor program. With more than 740 career wins, he is Baylor's all-time leader in wins in any sport.

Smith specializes as a pitching coach and has sent dozens of his hurlers into the pros. Among them is Ryan LaMotta; from 2003-06, LaMotta went 21-16 for Baylor with a 3.29 ERA.

The 2006 Bears landed in the NCAA Tournament, and LaMotta got an unusual "start" in the first game of the Houston Regional against 16th-ranked Arizona State. Senior Cory VanAllen originally started the game, but rain halted play in the second inning. When play resumed the next day, Smith went with LaMotta.

The senior's appearance was the 111th of his career and tied the school record set by Zane Carter (2000-04). He went the distance, scattering eight hits over eight innings, striking out eight and walking only one. He gave up only one earned run in the 3-2 win.

If it had been up to Smith, however, LaMotta wouldn't have finished the game. With Baylor leading 3-1, State loaded the bases in the bottom of the ninth with one out. That brought Smith out

BEARS

of the dugout to make a pitching change.

But LaMotta emphatically waved his head coach off, and Smith turned around and returned to the dugout. LaMotta gave up a sacrifice fly and got a strikeout to end the game and earn the win.

"(Waving off Smith) was a bit of a subconscious decision, not a voluntary thought," LaMotta said afterwards. "I just felt like it was my game." He was, after all, the boss.

No matter what our line of work may be, we all have bosses; even if we're self-employed, we work for our customers or clients. One of the key aspects of being an effective boss is spelling out in detail exactly what is expected of those whom the boss directs.

Wouldn't it be helpful if our faith life worked that way, too? Wouldn't it be wonderful if we had a boss who tells us exactly what we are to do? Well, we do.

For Christians, our boss is Jesus, the one to whom all authority on this Earth has been given. As the king of the world, Jesus is the grandest and biggest boss of all. The last thing that boss did before he left us for a while was to deliver a set of instructions. Jesus told us we are to do three things: 1) go and make disciples everywhere; 2) baptize those disciples; and 3) teach those disciples.

There we have it, straight from the head man's mouth just as clear and as precise as we could want it. The real question is how well we are following our boss's instructions.

It didn't really come as a big surprise. I haven't ever had anybody look at me quite like that before. He wanted to win the game.
— Steve Smith on being waved off by Ryan LaMotta

The king of the world is our boss, and
he has told us exactly what he wants us to do.

PLAN AHEAD

Read Psalm 33:1-15.

"The plans of the Lord stand firm forever, the purposes of his heart through all generations" (v. 11).

Grant Teaff had a plan to help his team gain a psychological advantage in a hostile atmosphere. The fact that his strategy made the opposing coach angry didn't concern him at all.

On Sept. 27, 1975, the Bears were in Ann Arbor to take on No. 9 Michigan. Playing the Wolverines was tough enough, but Baylor's head man was keenly aware of just what an edge Michigan had playing in its legendary Big House. More than 100,000 frenetic fans would be cheering against the visitors.

The Bear coaches tirelessly studied film as they prepared for the game, looking for anything they could use to their advantage. Teaff found one in a most unlikely place: those 100,000+ fans. He told his players, "You're going to be pleasantly surprised, because when you enter the stadium in Michigan, there will be over 100,000 people cheering for you."

Teaff had noticed that the visiting team at Ann Arbor always took the field just ahead of the Wolverines, but that the two teams entered through the same tunnel. As soon as the visitors trotted onto the field, the home team burst out of the tunnel — to the accompaniment of a deafening roar.

So Teaff devised a simple plan to use that noise to his team's advantage: Baylor would take the field after Michigan did.

BEARS

Wolverine head coach Bo Schembechler was furious when he learned of Teaff's plan. He said Baylor had to take field when he said so. "It's not in the contract," Teaff replied. "We'll follow you."

The Bears took the field right behind the Wolverines, thus receiving "a standing ovation from 104,000 Michigan fans and 248 Baylor fans." Teaff's plan didn't hurt. Only a missed field goal in the last few seconds kept Baylor from winning the game, which ended in a 14-14 tie.

Successful living — like successful coaching — takes planning. You go to school to improve your chances for a better paying job. You use blueprints to build your home. You plan for retirement. You map out your vacation to have the best time. You even plan your children — sometimes.

Your best-laid plans, however, sometime get wrecked by events and circumstances beyond your control. The economy goes into the tank; a debilitating illness strikes; a hurricane hits. Life is capricious and thus no plans — not even your best ones — are foolproof.

But you don't have to go it alone. God has plans for your life that guarantee success as God defines it if you will make him your planning partner. God's plan for your life includes joy, love, peace, kindness, gentleness, and faithfulness, all the elements necessary for truly successful living for today and for all eternity. And God's plan will not fail.

A man without a plan doesn't have a future.
— TCU head football coach Gary Patterson

Your plans may ensure a successful life;
God's plans will ensure a successful eternity.

GOOD LUCK

Read Acts 1:15-25.

*"Then they prayed, 'Lord, you know everyone's heart.
Show us which of these two you have chosen.' . . . Then
they cast lots" (vv. 24, 25a).*

Sometimes it helps to get lucky with recruits. Kim Mulkey got lucky with most of the lineup for a national championship team.

When the Baylor women beat Michigan State 84-62 on April 5, 2005, for the national title, only two of the starters, senior center Steffanie Blackmon and junior Chameka Scott, came to Baylor the conventional way. The other three involved some luck.

In 2000, her first year at Baylor, Mulkey, never even gave Chelsea Whitaker a look. "It would have been a waste of our time," Mulkey said, to recruit the high school All-American. Baylor just wasn't a good enough program for Whitaker; she went to Virginia.

Then luck stepped in. After one season at UVa, Whitaker hurt her knee, and while she was recuperating she saw what was happening in Waco: a winning program with winners like Sheila Lambert and Danielle Crockrom. She also wanted to play for a coach who had been a point guard. So she transferred and was the starting point guard for the national champs.

The father of Jennifer Roberts, a Baylor assistant, tipped his daughter off about this "diamond in the rough" he was working with. She was an exchange student playing only her second year of organized basketball. Mulkey took about five minutes to make up her mind when she saw the player nobody had heard of. She was All-American and Big-12 Player of the Year Sophia Young.

In 2002, a woman strode into Mulkey's office. She had earned a doctorate at Baylor's Truett Seminary and had praised the coaching staff to her niece, who was born and raised in Italy by Nigerian parents and who was with her that day She was Abiola Wabara.

Whitaker, Young, Wabara — three starters on the championship team who wound up at Baylor with the help of a little luck.

Ever think sometimes that other people have all the luck? Some guy wins a lottery while you can't get a raise at work. The ball takes a lucky bounce the other team's way, and Baylor loses a game. If you have any luck to speak of, it's bad.

To ascribe anything that happens in life to luck, however, is to believe that random chance controls everything, including you. But here's the truth: Luck exists only as a makeshift explanation for something beyond our ken. Even when the apostles in effect flipped a coin to pick the new guy, they acknowledged that the lots merely revealed to them a decision God had already made.

It's true that we can't explain why some people skate merrily through life while others suffer in horrifying ways. We don't know why good things happen to bad people and vice versa. But none of it results from luck, unless, as the disciples did, you want to attribute that name to the force that does indeed control the universe; you know — the one more commonly called God.

Luck is what happens when preparation meets opportunity.
— Darrell Royal

A force does exist that is in charge of your life,
but it isn't luck; it's God.

SMART MOVE

Read 1 Kings 4:29-34; 11:1-6.

"[Solomon] was wiser than any other man. . . . As Solomon grew old, his wives turned his heart after other gods, and his heart was not fully devoted to the Lord his God" (vv. 4:31, 11:4).

What in the world was Art Briles doing swapping quarterbacks right then? He was just making a smart move, that's all.

The great promise of the 2009 season ended in the third game when Robert Griffin III suffered a torn ACL that required reconstructive surgery. In the same game, senior backup Blake Szymanski injured a shoulder, leaving the game and most of the season in the hands of redshirt freshman Nick Florence. As a senior in 2012, Florence would break the school single-season passing record and would be Honorable Mention All-America. At this point, though, he had barely taken any snaps at practice.

Thus, Briles called him over and asked quite seriously, "Nick, do you even know the plays?" The quarterback chuckled, said "yes, sir," and trotted onto the field.

The team dropped its first four Big 12 games before everything clicked for Florence against Missouri on Nov. 7. He set a school record by throwing for 427 yards that included three touchdowns.

Thus, with Baylor leading 33-29 late in the game and facing fourth-and-goal at the Missouri 1, Briles appeared to be making a really dumb move when he yanked Florence for Szymanski, who hadn't played in five weeks. Why did he do it? Because of Florence's jersey number. The head coach wanted 335-lb. defensive tackle Phil Taylor in as a fullback and an extra blocker. The problem was that his number was 11, the same as Florence's. Having the two on the field together meant a penalty.

So the switch was a really smart move, especially when Terrance Ganaway blasted in for a touchdown and Baylor won 42-30.

Remember that time you wrecked the car when you spilled hot coffee on your lap? That cold morning you fell out of the boat? The time you gave your honey a tool box for her birthday?

Formal education notwithstanding, we all make some dumb moves sometimes because time spent in a classroom is not an accurate gauge of common sense. Folks impressed with their own smarts often grace us with erudite pronouncements that we intuitively recognize as flawed, unworkable, or simply wrong.

A good example is the observation that great intelligence and scholarship are inherently incompatible with a deep and abiding faith in God. That is, the more we know, the less we believe. Any incompatibility occurs, however, only because we begin to trust in our own wisdom rather than the wisdom of God. We forget, as Solomon did, that God is the ultimate source of all our knowledge and wisdom and that even our ability to learn is a gift from God.

Not smart at all.

I don't hire anybody not brighter than I am. If they're not smarter than me, I don't need them.

— Bear Bryant

Being truly smart means trusting in God's wisdom rather than only in our own knowledge.

PAYBACK

Read Matthew 5:38-42.

"I tell you, Do not resist an evil person. If someone strikes you on the right cheek, turn to him the other also" (v. 39).

The Bears definitely had payback on their mind when they took on Kansas State in 2013. Consider it done.

On Oct. 1, 2011, Baylor was undefeated and ranked 15th in the nation when the schedule required a trip to Manhattan. "It was probably one of the loudest places we've ever played," said receiver Tevin Reese, a sophomore at the time. The Kansas State fans threw a wall of sound onto the field, and it turned the game around. The Bears led 35-26, but they "couldn't hear themselves talk in the fourth quarter. . . . Communication broke down and their explosive offense ground to a halt." The Wildcats scored ten unanswered points and pulled out a stunning 36-35 win.

So on Oct. 12, 2013, the Bears were undefeated and ranked 15th in the nation when they revisited Manhattan for the first time since that massive disappointment. Reese knew exactly what the Bears wanted out of the trip: payback. "It sets fire in your heart," he said about the loss. "Even though we beat them last year, we still remember two years ago when we lost. We want to prove to people we can win on the road."

The noisy crowd was on hand again, and once again the Wildcats weren't pushovers. In fact, K-State scored 15 points in the third quarter to rally and take a 25-21 lead. Memories of the nightmarish fourth quarter of two seasons before were thick. On this day, though, the Bears exorcised all those demons.

On the second play of the last quarter, quarterback Bryce Petty hit Reese with a 54-yard TD toss. Late in the game, senior running back Glasco Martin scored on a 21-yard run right up the middle. The final of 35-25 was on the scoreboard.

"I like the fact we faced a lot of adversity and got a win on the road," head coach Art Briles said. He liked the payback too.

The very nature of an intense rivalry is that the loser will seek payback for the defeat of the season before. But what about in life when somebody's done you wrong; is it time to get even?

The problem with revenge in real life is that it isn't as clear-cut as a scoreboard. Life is so messy that any attempt at revenge is often inadequate or, worse, backfires and injures you.

As a result, you remain gripped by resentment and anger, which hurts you and no one else. You poison your own happiness while that other person goes blithely about her business. The only way someone who has hurt you can keep hurting you is if you're a willing participant.

But it doesn't have to be that way. Jesus ushered in a new way of living when he taught that we are not to seek revenge for the personal wrongs and injuries we suffer. Let it go and go on with your life. What a relief!

We came up here two years ago in the same situation and the same circumstances, and didn't get away with a win.
— Art Briles after the 2013 win paid K-State back

Resentment over a wrong injures you, not the other person, so forget it -- just as Jesus taught.

THE FUNERAL

Read Romans 6:3-11.

"If we died with Christ, we believe that we will also live with him" (v. 8).

Baylor's Board of Trustees once made a decision that so outraged the students they held a mock funeral.

In *The History of Baylor Sports*, Alan J. Lefever recounts that in 1893, the *Baylor Literary* magazine received a letter addressed to the captain of the Baylor "base ball [*sic*] team." The editor smugly replied that no such captain existed because the school "did not waste its time with baseball or rowing." Baylor's men "put their energies instead into being part of one of the best military drill teams in the state."

Only two years later, this attitude had changed. A writer for the same magazine noted that Baylor had "waked up to the fact that unless she encourages athletic sports she will be numbered among the old monkish schools of a century ago."

Intercollegiate football at Baylor began in 1899 (See Devotion No. 1.), and the school fielded a football team each year through 1905. However, football "was brought to a screeching halt in the summer of 1906 by the Board of Trustees" with the passage of a resolution declaring simply "that the game of football be abolished at Baylor University." The decision was in response to the increasingly violent nature of the game. In 1905 alone, nineteen young men died from football-related injuries.

The Baylor student body wasn't too happy about the decision. The men demonstrated their displeasure with a mock funeral for football in the quadrangle. The inscription on a faux tombstone read, "Here lies our dear football, long may his ashes rest; he died by vote of the trustees and not by our request."

With changes that made the game safer, college football was saved. In the summer of 1907, the Baylor trustees reversed their action, and football returned to campus after a year's absence.

One day, unlike that fake funeral at Baylor in 1906, you'll have a real one, and you want it to be a good one. You want a decent crowd, you want folks to shed some tears, and you want some reasonably distinguished-looking types to say some very nice things about you. Especially if they're all true.

But have you ever been to a funeral where the deceased you knew and the deceased folks were talking about were two different people? Where everyone struggled to say something nice about the not-so-dearly departed? Or a funeral that was little more than an empty acknowledgement that death is the end of all hope. Sad, isn't it?

Exactly what makes a good funeral, one where people laugh, love, and remember warmly and sincerely amid their honest tears? Jesus does. His presence as a friend of the deceased transforms a mourning of death into a celebration of life.

Always go to other people's funerals; otherwise, they won't come to yours.

— *Yogi Berra*

Amid tears there is hope; amid death there is resurrection – if Jesus is at the funeral.

WE JUST DISAGREE

Read Romans 14:13-23.

"For the kingdom of God is not a matter of eating and drinking, but of righteousness, peace and joy in the Holy Spirit (v. 17).

As weird as it may sound, the rings the players received for the 2012 Holiday Bowl reflect a score different from the official one that's in all the record books. That's because Art Briles doesn't agree with it.

The Bears won their last four games of 2012 season to finish at 7-5 and land in San Diego. It was the program's third straight bowl game, a feat never before accomplished. The opponent was UCLA, and the 17th-ranked Bruins were favored.

They obviously shouldn't have been. By halftime, the outcome wasn't in doubt as Baylor led 35-10. With 188 yards for the night, Nick Florence broke RGIII's school single-season passing record. Lache Seastrunk rushed for 138 yards and a touchdown; Glasco Martin ran for 98 yards and scored three times.

The Bears' domination led to a final score of . . . . Well, there's some disagreement about that. Baylor led 49-19 when UCLA was credited with a touchdown as time expired. Video replays, however, clearly showed that the Bruin ball carrier never broke the plane of the goal line. Briles attempted to challenge the call but discovered to his dismay that the replay officials were nowhere to be found. They had packed up for the night.

So UCLA was allowed to keep the touchdown, kick the PAT, and establish an official final score of 49-26.

Briles never agreed with that tally. Months later, the players, coaches, and staff received impressive, diamond-encrusted rings personally designed by the head coach to commemorate the win. Proudly displayed on the rings was the final score: 49-19.

The only time folks haven't disagreed among themselves was when Adam roamed the garden alone. Since then – well, we just can't seem to get along.

That includes Christians, who have never exactly been role models for peaceful coexistence among themselves. Not only does the greater body of Christ always seem to be spatting and feuding, but discord within individual churches is so common-place that God uses church splits to grow his kingdom.

Why can't Christians get along? Perhaps it's because we take our faith so seriously, which is a good thing. But perhaps also, it's because – as Paul warned – we can't separate the important stuff from the trivial.

Following Christ is about achieving righteousness, joy, and peace, not about following arcane, arbitrary prescriptions for daily living or even worship. All too often we don't get along because the rules and traditions we espouse — and not Christ's love — govern our hearts and our faith.

[The replay officials] just left before the game was over, so we couldn't do anything.
— Art Briles on why he couldn't challenge UCLA's last touchdown

**Christians will never get along as long as we
worry about and harp on things that we shouldn't.**

UNEXPECTEDLY

Read Matthew 24:36-51.

"No one knows about that day or hour, not even the angels in heaven, nor the Son, but only the Father" (v. 36).

The Baylor men advanced to the Elite Eight of the NCAA Tournament for the first time in school history in 2010, but they had to overcome something totally unexpected to even get out of the first round.

Picked by the coaches to finish tenth in the league in a preseason poll, the Bears defied all expectations by tying for second place and winning a record 28 games. They then earned a No.-3 seed, the highest in school history, in the NCAA Tournament.

And promptly ran into an unexpected buzz saw.

The opponent was 14th-seeded Sam Houston State. The 25-7 Bearkats "shocked Baylor by coming out in a triangle-and-two defense after playing man-to-man most of the season." State's head coach conceded that his team had never played the defense before and it had been installed only two days before the game.

The plan was to take the ball out of the hands of Baylor guards LaceDarius Dunn and Tweety Carter. It worked. "When I started the game, they didn't even let me touch the ball," Dunn said.

As a result, the Bears were out of sync and frustrated for much of the game. They found themselves in a 55-55 tie with 3:48 left in the contest after State hit a layup. With the chance for the school's first postseason win since 1950 slipping away, the Bears suddenly pulled themselves together. Now expecting State's defense, they went on a 10-2 run fueled by Dunn's pass inside to Quincy Acy for a dunk with 2:29 left.

Dunn, who set a school record for points in a season, then got a steal and drove inside for a bucket. When Acy returned the favor by hitting Dunn inside for a dunk, State was done.

The Bears won 68-59 and advanced to the tournament's second round where, as expected, they beat Old Dominion.

Just like the Bears against Sam Houston State, we think we've got everything figured out and under control, and then something unexpected – like a new defense – happens. About the only thing we can expect from life with any certainty is the unexpected.

God is that way too, suddenly showing up to remind us he's still around. A friend who calls and tells you he's praying for you, a hug from your child or grandchild, a lone lily that blooms in your yard — unexpected moments when the divine comes crashing into our lives with such clarity that it takes our breath away and brings tears to our eyes.

But why shouldn't God do the unexpected? The only factor limiting what God can do in our lives is the paucity of our own faith. We should expect the unexpected from God, this same deity who caught everyone by surprise by unexpectedly coming to live among us as a man and who will return when we least expect it.

Obviously, the triangle-and-two affected us.
— BU head coach Scott Drew on the unexpected State defense

God continually does the unexpected,
like showing up as Jesus,
who will return unexpectedly.

RUN FOR IT

Read John 20:1-10.

"Peter and the other disciple started for the tomb. Both were running, but the other disciple outran Peter and reached the tomb first" (vv. 3-4).

Robert Griffin III gained 2,254 yards on the ground in his four years at Baylor. Appropriately, therefore, he began his collegiate athletic career running.

For any college coach, national signing day is the most angst-ridden time of the year. Until that fateful fax comes through, all a coach can do is wait – and pray. In the case of the most important recruit Art Briles landed for his first class, however, no anxiety at all was involved. That's because Griffin was already on the Baylor campus for the 2008 spring semester.

An excellent student, Griffin had graduated from high school with honors midway through his senior year. He then enrolled at Baylor early to get a head start on what were then his three goals: get a college degree, win the starting job at quarterback, and try to qualify for the 2008 Summer Olympics.

Thus, despite being the most decorated and applauded football player in Baylor history, the first uniform Griffin wore as a Bear didn't have any pads at all. His first live competition in college was in a sprinter's suit; he ran hurdles that spring.

In 2007, Griffin had been named the Gatorade Texas Track & Field Athlete of the Year after setting a pair of state records in the hurdles and just missing a national record. As soon as spring football ended in 2008, Griffin trotted over to the school track and took off running. He won both the Big 12 gold medal and the NCAA Midwest Regional in the 400-meter hurdles. Then he placed third in the NCAA Outdoor Championships.

That landed him a spot in the U.S. Olympic Trials where he finished eleventh, one spot short of making the finals. Griffin had an interesting perspective on the disappointment: "Had I qualified for the Olympics, I might not have ever played football."

Hit the ground running — every morning that's what you do as you leave the house and re-enter the rat race. You run errands; you run though a presentation; you give someone a run for his money; you always want to be in the running and never run-of-the-mill.

You're always running toward something, such as your goals, or away from something, such as your past. Many of us spend much of our lives foolishly attempting to run away from God, the purposes he has for us, and the blessings he is waiting to give us.

No matter how hard or how far you run, though, you can never outrun yourself or God. God keeps pace with you, calling you in the short run to take care of the long run by falling to your knees and running for your life — to Jesus — just as Peter and the other disciple ran that first Easter morning.

On your knees, you run all the way to glory.

Not bad for an 18-year-old who should have been going to his senior prom.
— Writer Nick Eatman on Robert Griffin III's track exploits in 2008

You can run to eternity by going to your knees.

FOR ALL YOU KNOW

Read John 8:12-32.

"You will know the truth, and the truth will set you free"
(v. 32).

Frank Broyles had no clue what was going on, and he had a frustrating time finding out.

Former Baylor president and chancellor Abner McCall once said that it was only in 1947 that "Baylor really got serious about football." That's when Bob Woodruff came to town as the head football coach. He came from the Georgia Tech staff and brought Broyles with him as an assistant.

His first team went 5-5-0. The 1948 squad forged a 6-3-2 record that earned the program's first-ever bowl bid. They beat Wake Forest 20-7 in the Dixie Bowl in Birmingham, Ala. Woodruff's 1949 team was even better. The Bears finished a 8-2, second in the conference, but didn't secure a bowl bid.

The highlight of the season came on Nov. 19 against SMU, the two-time defending conference champions. Baylor quarterback Adrian Burk, who led the nation in passing, tossed an 80-yard TD pass to back Dudley Parker on the first play from scrimmage, and a wild shoot-out in the Cotton Bowl was under way.

The excitable Broyles was in a scouting booth in the press box watching the teams trade scores. He left shortly before halftime to meet with the team in the locker room. To his consternation, as the press elevator crawled to the ground level, Broyles heard a huge roar from the crowd. When he reached the ground, he ran to the nearest ramp and grabbed the nearest fan. "What happened? What happened?" he shouted. "Those guys scored again," was the exasperated reply. An equally exasperated and still clueless Broyles then had to ask, "Yes, yes, but which ones?"

It may have been Baylor. The Bears won 35-26.

Unlike Frank Broyles against SMU, you may know the score, but there's still much you just flat don't know. Maybe it's the formula for the area of a cylinder or the capital of Myanmar. You may not know how paper is made from trees. Or how toothpaste gets into the tube. And can you honestly say you know how the opposite sex thinks?

Despite your ignorance about certain subjects, you manage quite well because what you don't know generally doesn't hurt you too much. In certain aspects of your life, though, ignorance is anything but harmless. Imagine, for instance, the consequence of not knowing how to do your job. Or of getting behind the wheel without knowing how to drive a car.

And in your faith life, what you don't know can have awful, eternal consequences. To willfully choose not to know Jesus is to be condemned to an eternity apart from God. When it comes to Jesus, knowing the truth sets you free; ignoring the truth enslaves you. With Jesus, ignorance is anything but bliss.

My sister's expecting a baby, and I don't know if I'm going to be an uncle or an aunt.
— *Former NBA player Chuck Nevitt*

**What you don't know may not hurt you
except when it comes to Jesus.**

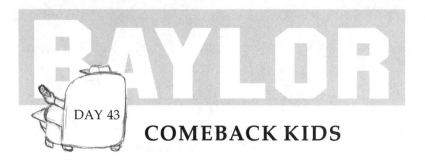

COMEBACK KIDS

Read Luke 23:26-43.

"Jesus answered him, 'I tell you the truth, today you will be with me in paradise'" (v. 43).

The 1980 Bears had to come back from a crushing loss, but they had a source of inspiration the likes of which they had never seen.

Baylor won its first seven games and grabbed a No.-10 national ranking. On Nov. 1, however, San Jose State upset the Bears 30-22. There followed what head coach Grant Teaff called "a week of misery" for the coaches and the players.

Dead ahead lay Arkansas, but "the players seemed dazed and unable to clear their minds of the devastating loss." Teaff called it the "oh, what might have been" syndrome. The team was focused on the defeat and not on the Razorbacks.

Thursday night, the coach made his weekly call to Kyle Woods. Woods had been a sophomore defensive back who, at a practice the season before, had fractured his neck and damaged his spine. The injury left him a quadriplegic.

Woods reminded Teaff he had not attended a game since his injury and asked if he could come Saturday. Steve Smith, a graduate assistant at the time who in 1995 was named Baylor's head baseball coach, volunteered to drive Woods to and from Waco.

Teaff found no emotion in the locker room before the game. He hadn't planned to do it, but he walked over, pushed Woods to the center of the room, and asked him if he had anything to say to his teammates. The room fell silent.

"Guys, it's simple," Woods said. "In life, setbacks have to be turned into comebacks." Then he dropped both hands to the arms of his wheelchair and somehow pushed himself to his feet. It was the first time he had stood since the accident and the last time he would ever stand again.

Inspired by Kyle Woods' glorious comeback, the Bears didn't lose again and won the Southwest Conference.

Life will have its setbacks whether they result from personal failures or from forces and people beyond your control. Being a Christian and a faithful follower of Jesus Christ doesn't insulate you from getting into deep trouble. Maybe financial problems suffocated you. A serious illness put you on the sidelines. Or your family was hit with a great tragedy.

Life is a series of victories and defeats. Winning isn't about avoiding defeat; it's about getting back up to compete again. It's about making a comeback of your own.

When you avail yourself of God's grace and God's power, your comeback is always greater than your setback. You are never too far behind, and it's never too late in life's game for Jesus to lead you to victory, to turn trouble into triumph.

As it was with the Bears of 1980 and the thief on the cross who repented, it's not how you start that counts; it's how you finish.

Kyle [Woods] clearly demonstrated his point to the team. [H]e had turned his tragic setback into an inspirational comeback.

— *Grant Teaff*

In life, victory is truly a matter of how you finish and whether you finish with Jesus at your side.

STRANGE BUT TRUE

Read Philippians 2:1-11.

"And being found in appearance as a man, he humbled himself and became obedient to death – even death on a cross!" (v. 7)

It's strange but true: Baylor once played a softball game that took more than seven years to complete.

Baylor first fielded an intercollegiate softball team in 1974. With deputy sheriff Bob Brock serving as head coach, the Bearettes of 1980 won the regional tournament and placed seventh in the national tournament. Paula Young won the first-ever Texas Association's Player of the Year Award in those pre-NCAA days.

As the 1988 season drew to a close, the decision was made to drop softball in favor of women's golf. The change was made in part because only one other Southwest Conference school played softball at the time while five others fielded women's golf teams. Young, the softball head coach, simply took over the golf team.

On April 27, the squad played Sam Houston State in what was to be the program's final game. The official record lists the game as a 7-2 loss, but it's actually not that simple. With two outs in the bottom of the last inning, the Baylor women walked off the field to symbolize that women's softball at the school was not over.

In 1994, the Baylor Board of Regents voted to resurrect the softball program. Thus, "the symbolic gesture that ended the 1988 season proved to be prophetic." The versatile Young left the golf team to head up the softball team again.

The decision was made to pick the program up right where it had left off. On Sept. 16, 1995, with some members of the original softball team present, Baylor and Sam Houston State began play with two outs in the last inning. The Lady Bears pushed a run across to make the final score of this strange softball game that lasted more than seven years 7-3.

Some things in life are so strange their existence can't really be explained. How else can we account for the sport of curling, tofu, that people go to bars hoping to meet the "right" person, the proliferation of tattoos, and the behavior of teenagers? Isn't it strange that today we have more ways to stay in touch with each other yet are losing the intimacy of personal contact?

And how strange is God's plan to save us? Think a minute about what God did. He could have come roaring down, destroying and blasting everyone whose sinfulness offended him, which, of course, is pretty much all of us. Then he could have brushed off his hands, nodded the divine head, and left a scorched planet in his wake. All in a day's work.

Instead, God came up with a totally novel plan: He would save the world by becoming a human being, letting himself be humiliated, tortured, and killed, thus establishing a kingdom of justice and righteousness that will last forever.

It's a strange way to save the world – but it's true.

We are thrilled to have Baylor softball back.
— Deann Duke, assistant athletic marketing director

**It's strange but true: God allowed himself
to be killed on a cross to save the world.**

HOMEBODIES

Read 2 Corinthians 5:1-10.

"We . . . would prefer to be away from the body and at home with the Lord" (v. 8).

Waco and Baylor just weren't home to Levi Norwood – until he realized they were the places where his faith could grow the most.

While he did catch 40 passes in 2012, Norwood was more known for his kick returns. That changed in 2013 when receiver Tevin Reese went down for the season. The junior then "quietly emerged as one of the Bears' biggest weapons," a dual threat with his receptions and his returns. He had 47 catches, trailing only Antwan Goodley's 71. He underwent wrist surgery and missed some games in 2014 but still finished his career in the top ten in all BU career kick return categories.

Proudly watching his son emerge as one of the team's most versatile players was Brian Norwood, BU's associate head coach. Because of his father's vocation, Levi was accustomed to moving while he was growing up. He wasn't surprised when his dad left Penn State in 2007 after seven seasons in Happy Valley to reunite with Art Briles, whom he had coached with at Texas Tech.

Levi also wasn't too happy about leaving his high school. He did manage a little excitement about the newness of it all — and then he arrived in Waco. "I got down here and the food was different, the people were different, the weather was different, the landscape — there's no mountains or hills here," he recalled.

BEARS

The youngest Norwood son adjusted, but that didn't mean he particularly wanted to stay. Thus, in 2010 during his senior year, he signed with Penn State; he was headed home again.

Or maybe not. Norwood found something "bigger than football, bigger than family [t]hat was more important to me than going up to Penn State." Just what was it? He realized that the place that gave him the best chance to grow his faith was Baylor.

Penn State released him and he stayed home.

Home is not necessarily a matter of geography. It may be that place you share with your spouse and your children, whether it's Texas or Pennsylvania. You may feel at home when you return to Waco, wondering why you were so eager to leave in the first place. Maybe the home you grew up in still feels like an old shoe, a little worn but comfortable and inviting.

It is no mere happenstance that among the circumstances of life that we most abhor is that of being homeless. That dread results from the sense of home God planted in us. Our God is a God of place, and our place is with him.

Thus, we may live a few blocks away from our parents and grandparents or we may relocate every few years, but we will still sometimes feel as though we don't really belong no matter where we are. We don't; our true home is with God in the place Jesus has gone ahead to prepare for us. We are homebodies and we are perpetually homesick.

It took a couple years for me to adjust.
— Levi Norwood on his new home, Waco

**We are continually homesick for our real home,
which is with God in Heaven.**

DAY 46

NO GUARANTEES

Read James 4:13-17.

"What is your life? You are a mist that appears for a little while and then vanishes" (v. 14b).

Steffanie Blackmon thought she was lightheaded because she hadn't eaten much that day. That was shortly before she collapsed, her heart stopped, and the doctors told the family to call their pastor in.

In May 2004, Steffanie, the Bears' junior All-American center, and her twin sister, Tiffanie, a Baylor post player sidelined by surgery, were riding together when Steffanie suddenly slumped over and began convulsing.

The convulsions continued at a nearby hospital, and Steffanie's heart stopped several times. Doctors used CPR to revive her and inserted a pacemaker to keep her heart beating. They advised the Blackmon family to call their pastor.

But she survived. After only three days, Steffanie was released from the hospital, very much alive and well. She even left her pacemaker behind.

She was diagnosed with a condition that causes a temporary loss of consciousness. It is usually harmless but, as in Steffanie's case, can be life-threatening.

After that one incident, she picked her life up again right where it had left off. As a senior forward, she was a key component of the 2005 drive to the national championship, making the NCAA

All-Tournament Team. She received no special attention from the Baylor trainers, just always making sure she had plenty of food and water. She finished her career as Baylor's all-time leader in blocked shots (a record broken by Brittany Griner and Danielle Wilson) and is fifth all-time in points scored.

The brush with death drew the Blackmon family closer together. "When Steffanie got sick, the love we had for one another showed," Tiffanie said. "I didn't want to lose her."

We all know that life is precious and precarious, fragile and fleeting. We manage to remain somewhat sane for the most part by tucking that depressing knowledge into a dark corner of our mind from which it only occasionally escapes.

One ironic result of that self-defense mechanism is that we often take God's priceless gift of life for granted. As Steffanie Blackmon's scary incident illustrates, though, life can end at any moment, no matter how young or how old we are.

This stark fact means that our life is in God's hands, not ours. The notion of being in control is an illusion born of our arrogance. We should never assume we have plenty of time to commit our lives to Jesus, to spend precious time with those we love, or to do the right thing in response to God's call.

We should live for today – but not for the useless baubles of this world. Rather, we should live today for God. Then, no matter when our life ends, we will receive God's guarantee of eternity.

We thought we would lose her.
— *Stan Blackmon on his daughter Steffanie*

**We should live today for God because
he guarantees eternity, not tomorrow.**

DAY 47

TRICK PLAYS

Read Acts 19:11-20.

"The evil spirit answered them, 'Jesus I know, and I know about Paul, but who are you?'" (v. 15)

The Bears once pulled a trick on TCU with a little tomfoolery involving the uniform.

As they often did before TCU left Waco and moved to Fort Worth after the school's main building burned in 1910, the two schools played each other three times in football in 1908. TCU won the first two games, and the schools agreed to a third contest on Thanksgiving Day.

TCU led 8-6 at halftime, but then Baylor "downright hungry for a victory over the Frogs, did an unusual thing" in an effort to confuse the opposition. John Fouts, Baylor's star left end, put on blue stockings — blue was a TCU color at the time — but kept on his Baylor gray jersey. After the second-half kickoff, Fouts ran to the Baylor sideline and snatched off his jersey. He revealed a blue one that, like his stockings, matched TCU's uniforms. He then re-joined his teammates on the field, creating the confusing illusion that TCU had furnished Baylor with one of its players.

Needless to say, TCU players and coaches were livid at what was perceived as a lowdown trick. They objected, but Baylor captain Babe Gantt "smilingly observed there was no law against it and demurred."

The trick must have worked. The Bears outscored TCU 17-0 in

the last half to win going away 23-8. The report of the game said Baylor's chicanery created widespread "bitterness and confusion" among the TCU team and its fans. The game left all of Waco in an uproar that evening.

For a long while, the account of Fouts' trickery could be found only in TCU's historical accounts. For some time, Baylor's history omitted any reference to what was called "Mr. Fouts' strip act."

Scam artists are everywhere — and they love trick plays. An e-mail encourages you to send money to some foreign country to get rich. That guy at your front door offers to resurface your driveway at a ridiculously low price. A TV ad promises a pill to help you lose weight without diet or exercise.

You've been around; you check things out before deciding. The same approach is necessary with spiritual matters, too, because false religions and bogus Christian denominations abound. The key is what any group does with Jesus. Is he the son of God, the ruler of the universe, and the only way to salvation? If not, then what the group espouses is something other than the true Word of God.

The good news about Jesus does indeed sound too good to be true, but the only catch is that there is no catch. When it comes to salvation through Jesus Christ, there's no trick lurking in the fine print. There's just the truth, right there for you to see.

When you run trick plays and they work, you're a genius. But when they don't work, folks question your sanity.

— *Bobby Bowden*

God's promises through Jesus sound too good to be true, but the only catch is that there is no catch.

THE BIG MO

Read 2 Chronicles 7:11-22.

"If my people, . . . will humble themselves and pray and seek my face and turn from their wicked ways, then will I hear from heaven and will forgive their sin" (v. 14).

Zero. If possible, less than zero. That's exactly how much momentum the Bears had. So all they did was win the game.

On Friday night, Sept. 2, 2011, the 14th-ranked Horned Frogs of TCU came into Floyd Casey Stadium and promptly got blown out — at least for a while. Robert Griffin shredded a defense that had led the nation for the last three seasons. On his way to throwing for 359 yards and five touchdowns, Griffin led the Bears to a 47-23 lead after the third quarter.

In the first half, Griffin tossed touchdown throws of 28 and 35 yards to Kendall Wright and one of 14 yards to Jordan Najvar. The Bears led 34-23 at the break and kept all the momentum with a pair of touchdowns receptions in the third quarter by junior wide receivers Lanear Simpson and Terrance Williams.

Game over. Uh, not quite.

As happens so often in football games, for some inexplicable reason, Ole Mo decided to step across the field to the other sideline. Suddenly, the Frogs caught fire. They blitzed the Bears for 25 straight points in the fourth quarter. A field goal with 4:27 on the clock left the stunned Bears trailing 48-47.

They may have been in shock, but they still believed. "I never saw any doubt there on the sideline, even when it got bad there in the fourth quarter," head coach Art Briles said.

Battling the clock, the TCU defense, and the lack of momentum, the Bears marched 60 yards after the kickoff. Aaron Jones booted a 37-yard field goal with 1:04 remaining, and junior safety Mike Hicks stole a Frog pass with 2 seconds left to clinch the 50-48 win.

Unlike a football game, momentum in real life usually doesn't happen suddenly. Any small business owner can speak of the early struggles before his enterprise became successful. We build our careers over the decades, moving up from entry-level positions. It's an old truism that maintaining success is harder than getting it; that is, keeping our momentum requires effort.

This is true in our faith lives also. We are all called by God to spiritual greatness, to a life of achieving extraordinary things for him that in turn spills over into achievements in other areas of our daily lives. Too many of us don't attain it, however. We may start out on fire for the Lord, but we sputter and fall short, overwhelmed by the challenges before us. We lose our momentum.

Even with our dreams surrendered, our lives stagnant, and our hopes dashed, we have a ready answer. We can do exactly what Solomon was told long ago: Turn back to God. We can intentionally choose God's direction for our lives and turn back to the godly lifestyle that established our momentum in the first place.

That last drive was a big-time deal because it's not easy to do when you have zero momentum.
— Art Briles on the game-winning drive vs. TCU

**With our lives going nowhere, we can turn
back to God for direction and momentum.**

MEMORY LOSS

Read 1 Corinthians 11:17-29.

"[D]o this in remembrance of me" (v. 24).

The 1944-45 Baylor basketball season was one to forget. What happened after that, however, was something to remember.

After the 1942-43 season, head coach Bill Henderson and the best basketball players were away at war. Unlike both football and baseball, however, the basketball program managed to soldier on despite the heavy attrition.

As Alan J. Lefever records it, the players on the two Baylor teams of 1943-44 and 1944-45 were "mostly preachers and people who couldn't get in the service." The undermanned squad that latter season "faced an apparently insurmountable challenge."

The only winless basketball season in Baylor history resulted. The team went 0-17 overall, 0-12 in the conference, suffering a series of lopsided losses. "It must have been an absolutely dispiriting season for the Bears," wrote Randy Fiedler.

If that season was forgettable, however, no Baylor fan should forget that what happened in 1945-46 was "one of the greatest turnarounds in college basketball history." Henderson and a number of athletes were back from the war. He led a team of newcomers to a 25-6 record (the most wins in school history at the time) and the Southwest Conference championship. The team was the first in the program's history to advance to the NCAA Tournament.

BEARS

The turnaround got even more memorable two seasons later, as guard Jackie Robinson, the program's third All-America, led the 1947-48 team all the way to the national championship game. The Bears lost to Kentucky, but "a rousing crowd of thousands" didn't forget what they had done, meeting them in Waco and leading them on a parade through downtown.

Memory makes us who we are. Whether our memories appear as pleasant reverie about Baylor wins or unnerving nightmares about Baylor losses, they shape us and to a large extent determine both our actions and our reactions. Alzheimer's is so terrifying because it steals our memory from us, and in the process we lose ourselves. We disappear.

The greatest tragedy of our lives is that God remembers. In response to that photographic memory, he condemns us for our sin. Paradoxically, the greatest joy of our lives is that God remembers. In response to that memory, he came as Jesus to wash even the memory of our sins away.

God uses memory as a tool through which we encounter revival. At the Last Supper, Jesus instructed his disciples and us to remember. In sharing this unique meal with fellow believers and remembering Jesus and his actions, we meet Christ again, not just as a memory but as an actual living presence. To remember is to keep our faith alive.

I don't want them to forget Babe Ruth. I just want them to remember Hank Aaron.

— Hank Aaron

**Because we remember Jesus,
God will not remember our sins.**

PROVE IT!

Read Matthew 3.

"But John tried to deter him, saying, 'I need to be baptized by you, and do you come to me?'" (v. 14)

Baylor had a whole lot to prove in its 2012 season opener. Consider the skeptics won over.

The football program had a pair of successful seasons behind it as the 2012 campaign began. Seventeen wins and two bowl games had the players and their fans riding high and hoping for more. But a huge shadow cast itself across the program, creating some doubt that the success could continue: that of Robert Griffin III. He was gone, a Washington Redskin now. The Bears had to prove they could win without him.

Thus, the opener on Sunday, Sept. 2, against SMU was exactly what head coach Art Briles called it: "a big, big game for us." It was a contest that could serve as a springboard to more success or as a setback that could have lingering effects.

So the Bears went out and proved that they were a team to be reckoned with and that the success they had enjoyed was not a flash in the pan. Impressive on both sides of the ball, they buried an SMU team that had been to three straight bowl games 59-24.

Making his first start since stepping in for an injured Griffin in 2009, senior quarterback Nick Florence proved he could lead the team, throwing for 341 yards and four touchdowns. The Bears roared to a 45-10 lead before Florence sat down and turned the game over to Bryce Petty.

The defense was equally impressive, forcing three turnovers. Linebacker Eddie Lackey and safety Sam Holl intercepted passes, and senior safety Mike Hicks gobbled up an SMU fumble and zipped 66 yards for a third-quarter touchdown.

Briles knew what was at stake in this one. "We were eager and anxious and wanted to prove ourselves," he said. "We did that."

Like the Bears, you, too, have to prove yourself over and over again in your life. To your teachers, to that guy you'd like to date, to your parents, to your bosses, to the loan officer. It's always the same question: "Am I good enough?" Practically everything we do in life is aimed at proving that we are.

And yet, when it comes down to the most crucial situation in our lives, the answer is always a decisive and resounding "No!" Are we good enough to measure up to God? To deserve our salvation? John the Baptist knew he wasn't, and he was not only Jesus' relative but God's hand-chosen prophet. If he wasn't good enough, what chance do we have?

The notion that only "good" people can be church members is a perversion of Jesus' entire ministry. Nobody is good enough – without Jesus. Everybody is good enough – with Jesus. That's not because of anything we have done for God, but because of what he has done for us. We have nothing to prove to God.

We're going to keep this thing rolling at Baylor.
— Nick Florence on what the Bears proved against SMU

The bad news is we can't prove to God's satisfaction how good we are; the good news is that because of Jesus we don't have to.

LIVE ACTION

Read James 2:14-26.

*"Faith by itself, if it is not accompanied by action, is dead"
(v. 17).*

The Florida Gators talked a good game. The Baylor Lady Bears
played a better game. Advantage Baylor.

The 35-0 and top-seeded Lady Bears took on the 20-12 Florida
Gators on March 20, 2012, in the second round of the NCAA Tournament. Before the match-up, some of the Gators had their say,
apparently believing they should have been the favored team.

For instance, a Gator guard said she didn't see "anything
spectacular" in Baylor's 81-40 thrashing of UC Santa Barbara in
the tournament's opening round. Florida's post player declared
she wasn't worried about being matched up against Brittany
Griner. She had played some overseas ball, she said, and that
would serve her well in the game. "I think it's time to start talking
about Florida," barked another Gator. "You know, what they've
done and what they're going to do."

Once the game began, though, the talking ended, and so did
Florida's season. In a contest highlighted by the sixth dunk of
Griner's career, the Lady Bears whipped the Gators 76-57.

Griner had a game-high 25 points, but her dunk at the 18:10
mark of the second half brought the crowd to its feet and left the
Florida players speechless. Kimetria Hayden grabbed an offensive rebound, pivoted, and scooped a pass to Griner in the lane.

BEARS

She "cocked the ball back and hammered home a powerful right-handed slam." "I think it even intimidated Florida for a second," said junior forward/post player Destiny Williams. "They just stepped back and watched."

The Lady Bears led by nine at halftime before breaking the game open after Griner's slam. They shot 55 percent the last half and led by 20 with three minutes left.

The Gators did have something to say after the loss. During the on-court handshakes, they graciously urged the Lady Bears to "go win it all," which, of course, is exactly what they did.

Talk is cheap. Consider your neighbor or coworker who talks without saying anything, who makes promises she doesn't keep, who brags about his own exploits, who can always tell you how to do something but never shows up for the work. You know that speech without action just doesn't cut it.

That principle applies in the life of a person of faith too. Merely declaring our faith isn't enough, however sincere we may be. It is putting our faith into action that shouts to the world of the depth of our commitment to Christ.

Even Jesus didn't just talk, though he certainly did his share of preaching and teaching. Rather, his ministry was a virtual whirlwind of activity. As he did, so are we to change the world by doing. Anybody can talk about Jesus, but it is when we act for him that we demonstrate how much we love him.

Jesus Christ is alive; so should our faith in him be.

Don't talk too much or too soon.

— *Bear Bryant*

Faith that does not reveal itself in action is dead.

WEATHERPROOFED

Read Nahum 1:3-9.

"His way is in the whirlwind and the storm, and clouds are the dust of his feet" (v. 3b).

Grant Teaff once used the weather to such an advantage that an assistant from the opposing team admitted the game was over days before it began.

The Bears of 1985 went 9-3, beat LSU in the Liberty Bowl, and finished with a No.-17 national ranking. They began that season on Sept. 7 at home against Wyoming.

In August, Central Texas experienced a major heat wave that boasted frequent days with temperatures of 110 degrees. Teaff estimated that the temperature on the field inside Baylor Stadium was about 20 degrees hotter. He decided to pull off a little publicity stunt that he figured might help psych out the Cowboys, who were unaccustomed to such heat.

One afternoon, he had the Sports Information Director call the local media, and they gathered at the stadium's 50-yard line. Teaff emerged from the tunnel "wearing a chef's hat with a skillet in one hand and an egg in the other." He set the skillet on the rubberized surface separating the field from the stadium wall. He then said to the media folks, "Everyone says it's hot enough to fry an egg inside this stadium; let's see."

The head coach proceeded to kneel down by the skillet, crack open the egg, and drop it into the pan. The egg immediately

BEARS

began to sizzle while cameras flashed.

Not surprisingly, a photograph of Teaff frying that egg on the stadium turf went national, and the Laramie, Wyo., paper picked it up.

The Bears blasted Wyoming 39-18. After the game, one of the Cowboy assistant coaches confessed to a Baylor staffer, "The day Coach Teaff's picture frying that egg appeared in our paper, the game was over."

A thunderstorm washes away your golf game or the picnic with the kids. Lightning knocks out the electricity just as you settle in at the computer. A tornado interrupts your Sunday dinner and sends everyone scurrying to the hallway. A hurricane blows away your beach trip.

For all our technology and our knowledge, we are still at the mercy of the weather, able only to get a little more advance warning than in the past. The weather answers only to God. Rain and hail will fall where they want to and will be totally inconsiderate of something as important as a Baylor football game.

We stand mute before the awesome power of the weather, but we should be even more awestruck at the power of the one who controls it, a power beyond our imagining. Neither, however, can we imagine the depths of God's love for us, a love that drove him to die on a cross for us.

Well, yes, the pan was preheated. It was hot, but not that hot.
— Grant Teaff on his weather ploy

The power of the one who controls the weather is
beyond anything we can imagine,
but so is his love for us.

ANIMAL MAGNETISM

Read Psalm 139:1-18.

"For you created my inmost being; you knit me together in my mother's womb. I praise you because I am fearfully and wonderfully made" (vv. 13-14).

Some overexuberant Texas A&M cadets once did their football team a huge disservice: They kidnapped the Baylor bears.

The Aggies were ranked 13th in the nation when they sashayed into brand new Baylor Stadium on Oct. 28, 1950. With a powerful ground game, A&M had lost only once, and that by six points to an Oklahoma team that would win the national title. Under first-year head coach George Sauer, the Bears were 3-2.

Fever ran particularly high before this game because during the week several A&M cadets kidnapped Baylor's two cub mascots. As a result, the Baylor fans and student body and especially the players were fired up.

The Bears sure didn't start out like it, though. A&M scored on the first play of the game and hit a touchdown pass only a couple of minutes later for a quick 13-0 lead.

After that, though, the day — and the game — belonged to Baylor's junior quarterback, Larry Isbell. It was said of him that he "really came of age" this day, "proving to the Southwest Conference what a special talent he was." Isbell was a rarity in college athletics: a two-sport All-America. He earned the honor in football in 1951 and in baseball in 1952. Each year now the baseball

BEARS

team awards the Larry Isbell MVP trophy.

Isbell threw four touchdown passes that afternoon, ran the ball well, and punted six times for a 46-yard average. He rallied Baylor to a 27-20 win, and the Bears were sitting on the A&M 1-yard line when the game ended.

By then, the purloined cubs had been returned to their Waco home. The bearnappers wanted nothing more to do with them because the ursine critters had ripped to shreds the upholstery of their car's back seat.

Animals such as Joy and Lady, Baylor's current mascots, elicit our awe and our respect. Nothing enlivens a trip more than glimpsing turkeys, bears, or deer in the wild. Admit it: You go along with the kids' trip to the zoo because you think it's a cool place too. All that variety of life is mind-boggling. Who could conceive of bear, a walrus, a moose, or a prairie dog? Who could possibly have that rich an imagination?

But the next time you're in a crowd, look around at the parade of faces. Who could come up with the idea for all those different people? For that matter, who could conceive of you? You are unique, a masterpiece who will never be duplicated.

The master creator, God Almighty, is behind it all. He thought of you and brought you into being. If you had a manufacturer's label, it might say, "Lovingly, fearfully, and wonderfully handmade in Heaven by #1 -- God."

The bears enjoy what they do here; we in turn respect and love them.
— 'Mascot History' on Baylor's live bears

You may consider some painting or a magnificent animal a work of art; the real masterpiece is you.

THE RIGHT MAN

Read Exodus 3:1-12.

"So now, go. I am sending you to Pharaoh to bring my people the Israelites out of Egypt" (v. 10).

Art Briles was obviously the right man to lead the Baylor football program, but he wasn't the first choice among many boosters and alums.

After the 2007 season, the Bears were once again in need of a new coach. Fifteen years had passed since the legendary Grant Teaff had roamed the sidelines, and the program was still trying to replace him. This time the fan base knew what it wanted: a name coach who would make a splash. Moreover, the supporters knew who the right man for the job was: Mike Singletary.

Singletary is a Baylor legend, a three-time All-American linebacker who still holds the school records for career tackles (662) and tackles in a season (232). He won the Davey O'Brien Award in 1979 and 1980 as the most outstanding player in the Southwest.

Baylor AD Ian McCaw wasn't sure, however, that Singletary was the right fit for the school, but the pressure was too great. Singletary was coaching with the San Francisco 49ers, so McCaw flew to California for an interview. Both sides came away from the meeting convinced the Baylor job wasn't the best option. "It just seemed like [Singletary] was on the NFL track and really wasn't what we were looking for," McCaw said.

So he turned his attention elsewhere, assisted by a consulting firm. "The one name, in [their] homework and my homework, that kept rising to the top was Art Briles," McCaw said. Unlike Singletary, however, would the head coach at Houston, whom McCaw had never met, be the right man for the job?

The two met on Nov. 26 in Dallas and spoke for three hours. McCaw came away convinced he had found his man. Two days later, Briles was announced as the new head football coach at Baylor. The right man was on his way to Waco.

What do you want to be when you grow up? Somehow you are supposed to know the answer to that question when you're a teenager, the time in life when common sense and logic are at their lowest ebb. Long after those halcyon teen years are left behind, you may make frequent career changes. You chase the job that gives you not just financial rewards but also some personal satisfaction and sense of accomplishment.

God, too, wants you in the right job, one that he has designed specifically for you. Though Moses protested that he wasn't the right man, he was indeed God's anointed one, the right man to do exactly what God needed done.

There's a little Moses in all of us. Like him, we shrink before the tasks God calls us to. Like him also, we have God-given abilities, talents, and passions. The right man or women for any job is the one who works and achieves not for self but for the glory of God.

He knew Briles was the right leader for the Baylor football program.
— Writer Nick Eatman on Ian McCaw's interview with Art Briles

**Working for God's glory and not your own
makes you the right person for the job,
no matter what it may be.**

TRAGEDY

Read Job 1, 2:1-10.

"In all this, Job did not sin by charging God with wrongdoing" (v. 1:22).

Each year, Baylor freshmen remember one of the first great tragedies in college sports.

Rain was falling as first-year head coach Ralph Wolf and his basketball players boarded a chartered bus on Jan. 22, 1927, for a ride to Austin and a game against the University of Texas. Along the way, debris from the road sprayed the windshield of the bus, hampering the bus driver's vision.

In Round Rock, the bus neared a railroad crossing obscured by the weather and several buildings. Those buildings also hid a speeding northbound passenger train that blew its whistle as it neared the crossing. No one on the bus heard it.

Wolf saw the train and alerted the driver. He responded quickly, but simply didn't have enough time. The train struck the rear of the bus, killing ten of the 21 players, coaches, and fans aboard.

James Clyde "Abe" Kelly, captain-elect of Baylor's 1927 football team, also saw the train coming. Just before the collision, he pushed teammate Weir Washam out of a window, saving his life. Kelly was one of the ten who died.

The others who did not survive the collision were William Winchester, W.E. Murray, Merle Dudley, Sam Dillow, Jack Castellaw, Ivey Foster, Bob Hailey, R.L. Hannah, and James Walker. In a column the next day, the *Waco Times-Herald* referred to the victims of the tragedy as the Immortal Ten.

And so are they remembered. Each year, Baylor freshmen are told their story anew and participate in a candlelight remembrance ceremony. In 2007, a longheld dream came true when a memorial to the Immortal Ten was erected on campus.

While we may receive them in varying degrees, suffering and tragedy are par for life's course. What we do with tragedy when it strikes us determines to a great extent how we live the rest of our lives.

We can – in accordance with the bitter suggestion Job's wife offered — "Curse God and die" — or we can trust God and live. That is, we can plunge into endless despair or we can lean upon the power of a transcendent faith in an almighty God who offers us hope in our darkest hours.

We don't have to understand tragedy; we certainly don't have to like it or believe there's anything fair about it. What we must do in such times, however, is trust in God's all-powerful love for us and his promise that all things will work for good for those who love him.

In choosing a life of ongoing trust in God in the face of our suffering, we prevent the greatest tragedy of all: that of a soul being cast into Hell.

The monument [honoring the Immortal Ten] recalled these lost sons of Baylor and rekindled the Baylor spirit they have come to symbolize.
— *Writer Alan J. Lefever*

Tragedy can drive us into despair and death or into the life-sustaining arms of almighty God.

GREAT EXPECTATIONS

Read John 1:43-51.

"'Nazareth! Can anything good come from there?'
Nathanael asked" (v. 46).

Pass-happy offense run by a pass-happy former high school coach in a pass-happy league." Such are the expectations of many folks when they consider Baylor football, but they may not get what they expect.

"It's kind of a misconception we appreciate," head coach Art Briles once said about the notion that the Bears are nothing but a bunch of football airheads. Of course, 70-63 is an actual football score from 2012 and not a Bear basketball final. And true, Baylor gains a whole lot of yards through the air. In 2012, the Bears finished fourth in the nation in passing; in 2013, they were fifth.

But the 2012 season turned around when the Bears turned to a more balanced offense. They were only 3-4 on Nov. 3 when Lache Seastrunk rushed for 103 yards on 17 carries in a win over Kansas. He never gained fewer than 91 yards in a game after that, and Baylor didn't lose again. The Bears wound up leading the Big 12 in rushing with 3,012 yards.

They led the nation in total offense in 2013 as they marched and flew to the Big 12 title, achieving a balance no other team could equal. Behind junior Bryce Petty, they threw for 4,668 yards, fifth in the nation. But Seastrunk rushed for 1177 yards while Shock Linwood ran for 881 yards and Glasco Martin added another 509 yards. Baylor totaled 3,376 yards on the ground and finished thirteenth in the nation in rushing.

The beat kept on in 2014. The Bears finished fourth in the country in total offense behind an air attack that garnered 4,757 yards and a strong ground game that added another 2,802 yards.

Baylor does pass the ball, but not as much as folks might expect. In truth, the Bears love to run about as much as they love to throw.

The blind date your friend promised would look like Brad Pitt or Jennifer Aniston but resembled a Munster or Cousin Itt. Your vacation that went downhill after the lost luggage. Often your expectations are raised only to be dashed. Sometimes it's best not to get your hopes up; then at least you have the possibility of being surprised.

Worst of all, perhaps, is when you realize that you are the one not meeting others' expectations. The fact is, though, that you aren't here to live up to what others think of you. Jesus didn't; in part, that's why they killed him. But he did meet God's expectations for his life, which was all that really mattered.

Because God's kingdom is so great, God does have great expectations for any who would enter, and you should not take them lightly. What the world expects from you is of no importance; what God expects from you is paramount.

People think of us as a passing football team, but if it's time to get dirty, we're going to get dirty.
— Art Briles

You have little if anything to gain from meeting the world's expectations of you; you have all of eternity to gain from meeting God's.

CASE OF THE NERVES

Read Mark 5:1-20.

"What do you want with me, Jesus, Son of the Most High God? Swear to God that you won't torture me!" (v. 7)

Jackie Robinson was nervous about meeting England's King George VI, but that didn't keep him from correcting the ruler's misunderstanding about Texas.

In 1948, Robinson became the third All-American in BU basketball history (after Hubert "Hub" Kirkpatrick in 1938 and Earl "Pete" Creasey in 1939). The '48 team won the SWC championship and advanced to the finals of the NCAA Tournament. With Robinson hampered by a bad knee, Kentucky won 58-42.

On the way down from his New York hotel room the morning after the championship game, Robinson glanced down at a pile of newspapers the doorman sold each day. A *New York Times* headline declared "U.S. Olympic Team Chosen" with a subhead that read "Lumpp, Robinson added." That's how Robinson found out he had made the 1948 U.S. Olympic team.

In London, the Americans won the gold, challenged seriously only by Argentina. The U.S. won that game 59-57 with Robinson scoring six points in the closing minutes. He kept the game ball.

Members of the Olympic teams were treated to tea with the royal family at Buckingham Palace with Robinson chosen to represent the U.S. men. He was "awfully nervous" about meeting King George VI, Queen Elizabeth, and their daughter, the future

BEARS

Queen Elizabeth II. In the formal reception line, Robinson shook hands with the king. "He couldn't have been nicer," he recalled.

Sometime later in a more informal setting, Robinson and some other athletes, including a swimmer from California, were chatting with the king when he exclaimed, "California. That's where the biggest and best come from!" Nervous no longer, Robinson piped up to correct the ruler of the British Empire by telling him that the biggest and the best came from Texas, not California.

Pressured situations, like Jackie Robinson's meeting the king, often make us nervous. Making a speech, for instance. Or being in the presence of a person we'd like to ask out.

We probably rarely if ever consider the possibility that we make other people nervous. Who in the world could be intimidated by us? Try this on for starters: Satan himself. Yep, that very demon of darkness that Hollywood repeatedly portrays as so powerful that goodness is helpless before him. That's the one.

But we can make Satan nervous only if we stand before him with the power of Jesus Christ at our disposal. As Christians, we seem to understand that our basic mission is to further Jesus' kingdom and change the world through emulating him in the way we live and love others. But do we appreciate that in truly living for Jesus, we are daily tormenting the very devil himself?

Satan and his lackeys quake helplessly in fear and nervousness before the power of almighty God that is in us through Jesus.

Whoa, Sir, I'm from Texas.
— *Jackie Robinson to King George VI*

**Nervous and apprehensive -- so stands Satan
in the presence of a follower of Jesus.**

CLOTHES HORSE

Read Genesis 37:1-11.

"Israel loved Joseph more than all his children, because he was the son of his old age: and he made him a coat of many colours" (v. 3 KJV).

The truth came out in New York City: Apparently Robert Griffin III won the 2011 Heisman Trophy as the nation's best college football player in part because of his socks.

On Saturday, Dec. 11, 2011, Baylor's junior quarterback joined "the most exclusive club in college sports" when he was presented with the Heisman Trophy. The award capped off a sensational junior season in which Griffin led the nation in passing efficiency by completing 72.4 percent of his throws for 3,998 yards and 36 touchdowns. He quarterbacked the Bears to a 9-3 record in the regular season, the school's best mark in 25 years.

"This award is the result of Robert's dedication and discipline and the support of our team and football program," said Baylor's head football coach Art Briles. Griffin revealed, however, that something else may have had a hand in his success. Dressed in a black pinstripe suit, during the ceremony he lifted a pants leg to uncover a pair of Superman socks complete with a red cape.

Just one pair in Griffin's collection of goofy socks that often feature cartoon characters, the Superman pair turned up again the Monday night after the Heisman ceremony when Griffin was a guest on David Letterman's late show. During a separate interview with *ESPN*, Griffin sported a pair of Elmo socks. He once said that he had enough pairs of the whimsical socks in his collection to wear a different set every day for two months. He had at various times displayed the Cookie Monster, Angry Birds, and SpongeBob SquarePants.

None of those, however, were quite appropriate for the Heisman ceremony. That night indeed required a dash of Superman.

Contemporary society proclaims that it's all about the clothes. Buy that new suit or dress, those new shoes, and all the sparkling accessories, and you'll be a new person.

The changes are only cosmetic, though; under those clothes, you're the same person. Consider Joseph, for instance, prancing about in his pretty new clothes; he was still a spoiled little tattletale whom his brothers detested enough to sell into slavery.

Jesus never taught that we should run around half-naked or wear only second-hand clothes from the local mission. He did warn us, though, against making consumer items such as clothes a priority in our lives. A follower of Christ seeks to emulate Jesus not through material, superficial means such as wearing special clothing like a robe and sandals.

Rather, the disciple desires to match Jesus' inner beauty and serenity — whether the clothes the Christian wears are the sables of a king or the rags of a pauper.

When you go to a Heisman ceremony, you should wear your best suit, shoes and socks.
— Robert Griffin III, explaining his Superman socks in New York City

Where Jesus is concerned, clothes
don't make the person; faith does.

MAKE NO MISTAKE

Read Mark 14:66-72.

"Then Peter remembered the word Jesus had spoken to him: 'Before the rooster crows twice you will disown me three times.' And he broke down and wept" (v. 72).

With their season in the balance, all the Bears had to do was get the ball in bounds -- and they blew it.

After a horrid 2-8 start in Big 12 play, the 2013-14 Baylor men's basketball team had to close with a flourish to have any hopes of grabbing a spot in the NCAA Tournament. Three straight wins kept those hopes alive, but they were still fighting for their tournament lives when they hosted Oklahoma State on Feb. 17.

After, trailing by ten points, the Bears rallied, taking the lead on a dunk by sophomore center Isaiah Austin with five minutes to play. They led 58-55 with only 3.5 seconds on the clock. The Bears had the ball out of bounds; all they had to do to keep their drive to the tournament on track was get the ball in bounds and run out the clock or hit a free throw when they were fouled.

Easier said than done. To the home crowd's horror, the Cowboys stole the attempted inbounds pass and nailed a trey at the buzzer. Thanks to a huge mistake, the Bears found themselves headed into overtime rather than celebrating a big win.

They recovered from that blunder, though, thanks in large part to senior forward Cory Jefferson, who led the team in scoring and rebounding. He was named Third-Team All-Big 12.

BEARS

Jefferson started the overtime by nailing a three and finished it with a pair of free throws. In a game they had to have, the Bears won 70-64. Jefferson wound up with 25 points and 13 rebounds.

The game indeed turned out to be a big one for the season. The team closed by winning seven of its last eight games to post a 21-10 record and earn a spot in the Big Dance. The Bears advanced to the Sweet Sixteen before losing.

It's distressing but it's true: Like Baylor's basketball teams and Simon Peter, we all make mistakes. Only one perfect man ever walked on this earth, and no one of us is he. Some mistakes are just dumb. Like locking yourself out of your car or falling into a swimming pool with your clothes on.

Other mistakes are more significant and carry with them the potential for devastation. Like heading down a path to addiction. Committing a crime. Walking out on a spouse and the children.

All these mistakes, however, from the momentarily annoying to the life-altering tragic, share one aspect: They can all be forgiven in Christ. Other folks may not forgive us; we may not even forgive ourselves. But God will forgive us when we call upon him in Jesus' name.

Thus, the twofold fatal mistake we can make is ignoring the fact that we will die one day and subsequently ignoring the fact that Jesus is the only way to shun Hell and enter Heaven. We absolutely must get this one right.

That's like getting punched in the gut.
— Baylor coach Scott Drew on the mistake that led to the tie at the end

**Only one mistake we make sends us to Hell
when we die: ignoring Jesus while we live.**

HURRY UP AND WAIT

Read Acts 1:1-14.

"Do not leave Jerusalem, but wait for the gift my Father promised, which you have heard me speak about" (v. 4).

Some patience and a lot of faith helped Bryce Petty wait — and wait and wait — for his chance to play for Baylor.

When Petty signed after the 2008 season, head coach Art Briles made it clear that he would wait years before he could lead the Bears since Robert Griffin III was just a sophomore. Petty "gray-shirted" in the fall of 2009 and joined the team in the spring of 2010. He waited in 2011 while Griffin won the Heisman Trophy and then waited some more in 2012 while Nick Florence broke Griffin's single-season passing record.

Though Petty appreciated that he was learning the nuances of Art Briles' spread attack and was growing as a quarterback the whole time, the waiting was never easy. "I'm not a very patient person," he admitted. "It doesn't matter if you're watching a Heisman Trophy winner; it's hard because you feel you can do it."

Petty relied on his faith and discussions with his parents to help him through the long, trying wait. A former youth pastor who counseled Petty consistently reminded him that God had a plan for his life and that his calling included being a great football player. "My faith has grown on and off the field," Petty said about this time.

Finally, almost four years after he had started his last football

BEARS

game, Petty's wait ended. He was the starter in the opener against Wofford on Aug. 31, 2013, and went on to quarterback the Bears to their greatest season ever: 11 wins, the Big 12 championship, and a BCS bowl. He was the Big 12 Offensive Player of the Year, accounting for an astounding 4,409 yards and 46 touchdowns.

For Petty and for Baylor fans, the long wait was worth it.

You rush to your doctor's appointment and wind up sitting in the appropriately named waiting room for an hour. You wait in the concessions line at a Baylor game. You're put on hold when you call a tragically misnamed "customer service" center. All of that waiting is time in which we seem to do nothing but feel the precious minutes of our life ticking away.

Sometimes we even wait for God. We have needs, and we call upon the Lord in our desperation and are disappointed when we perhaps get no immediate answer.

But Jesus' last command to his disciples was to wait. Moreover, the entire of our Christian life is spent in an attitude of waiting for Jesus' return. While we wait for God, we hold steadfast to his promises, we continue our ministry, we remain in communion with him through prayer and devotion.

In other words, we don't just wait; we grow stronger in our faith. Waiting for God is never time lost.

God has had his hand in my life. It's so evident through all the waiting for football to come together like it is now.
— *Bryce Petty during the 2013 season*

**Since God acts on his time and not ours,
we often must wait for him,
using the time to strengthen our faith.**

TOLD YOU SO

Read Matthew 24:15-31.

"See, I have told you ahead of time" (v. 25).

Billy Patterson may well have wanted to tell the Texas head coach "I told you so," but he had a whole delegation of Baylor fans who did it for him.

"Bullet" Bill Patterson quarterbacked the Bears for head coach Morley Jennings from 1936-38. In the offensive scheme of his day, he called the plays and was in reality a single and double wing tailback. He was the Southwest Conference MVP in 1937, a two-time all-conference back, and a second-team All-America in 1938. He threw two long touchdown passes and earned MVP honors in the 1939 East-West Shrine Game.

In the 20-14 defeat of defending SWC champion Arkansas in 1937, Patterson ran 71 yards for a touchdown, threw a pass for a 71-yard score, grabbed an interception, and then followed up with the game-winning touchdown pass. Three weeks later, he threw a long pass to All-SWC end Sam Boyd for a 6-0 win over TCU. The Frogs were led by Davey O'Brien, the first player west of the Mississippi River to win the Heisman Trophy.

Patterson had been outstanding in high school in Hillsboro. Some local folks had him all set to play for Texas, and so they arranged a meeting between Patterson and the Longhorn head coach at the Andrews Cafe in Hillsboro. Patterson showed up and waited around for a while but the Texas coach never came.

BEARS

Thus, Patterson wound up at Baylor. In his sophomore season, he led the Bears to three touchdowns in the fourth quarter and a thrilling 21-18 win over the Longhorns in Austin. He certainly would have been quite justified in telling the head coach who hadn't bothered to meet with him, "I told you so."

He didn't have to. A group from Hillsboro went to the Texas coach after the game and told him, "The kid who did so much in that last drive to beat you is the one you stood up in Hillsboro."

Don't you just hate it in when somebody says, "I told you so"? That means the other person was right and you were wrong; that other person has spoken the truth. You could have listened to that know-it-all in the first place, but then you would have lost the chance yourself to crow, "I told you so."

In our pluralistic age and society, many view truth as relative, meaning absolute truth does not exist. All belief systems have equal value and merit. But this is a ghastly, dangerous fallacy because it ignores the truth that God proclaimed in the presence and words of Jesus.

In speaking the truth, Jesus told everybody exactly what he was going to do: come back and take his faithful followers with him. Those who don't listen or who don't believe will be left behind with those four awful words, "I told you so," ringing in their ears and wringing their souls.

Whatever it is you are going to do in life, you are always going to have people waiting to say, 'I told you so.'
— *Football coach Jon Embree*

Jesus told us exactly what he has planned:
He will return to gather all the faithful to him.

DAY 62

ON CALL

Read 1 Samuel 3:1-18.

"The Lord came and stood there, calling as at the other times, 'Samuel! Samuel!' Then Samuel said, 'Speak, for your servant is listening'" (v. 10).

Nick Florence was called upon to make a sacrifice for the team such as few athletes are ever asked to do.

The Bears of 2011 were rolling on Nov. 26 when they made their way into Cowboys Stadium to take on Texas Tech. After a pair of losses in mid-season that had dropped them to 4-3, they had beaten Missouri, rallied to beat Kansas, and won a thriller against Oklahoma. (See Devotion No. 30.)

Tech was only 5-6, but the Red Raiders would not roll over. They needed the win to be bowl eligible. Also, Art Briles was 0-3 against the team from Lubbock.

Thus, it came as no surprise that Tech trailed only 31-28 at half-time. But Baylor was in trouble. Shortly before the break, Robert Griffin III suffered an apparent concussion. He was ready to play, but as Briles put it, "We got in at halftime, he had a little trouble remembering what was going on."

So the coaches took Griffin's helmet away from him. But who would replace the nation's total offensive leader? The obvious choice was backup Bryce Petty. (See Devotion No. 60.) Briles, however, decided the team would be better off on this day heading in another direction.

BEARS

He turned to Florence, a junior who was being redshirted so he could have two years of eligibility left. Playing the last half meant Florence would lose the whole season. "Whatever I can do to help the team, I'll do it," Florence told his coach. "If you need me, I'll play." "We need you, Nick," Briles replied.

So Florence played the final two quarters. He hadn't thrown a pass all season, but he was 9-for-12 with 151 yards and a pair of long touchdown throws. He led the Bears to a wild 66-42 win.

Florence didn't play another snap in 2011. Because he answered the call, his entire junior season consisted of two quarters.

A team player is someone who does whatever the coach calls upon him to do for the good of the team. Something quite similar occurs when God places a specific call upon a Christian's life.

This is much different, though, than sacrificing a season for a football team as Nick Florence did. The way many folks understand it is that answering God's call means going into the ministry, packing the family up, and moving halfway around the world to some place where folks have never heard of air conditioning, fried chicken, paved roads, or the Bears. Zambia. The Philippines. Cleveland even.

Not for you, no thank you. And who can blame you?

But God usually calls folks to serve him where they are. In fact, God put you where you are right now, and he has a purpose in placing you there. Wherever you are, you are called to serve him.

The team needed me right then. I've never regretted that decision.
— Nick Florence on answering the call for the Bears vs. Texas Tech

God calls you to serve him right now,
right where he has put you, wherever that is.

DAY 63

THE MOTHER LODE

Read John 19:25-30.

"Near the cross of Jesus stood his mother" (v. 25).

Kim Mulkey desperately wanted to throw some fire and brimstone at her team at halftime, but she couldn't. She had motherly duties to perform instead.

To her intense chagrin, Baylor's Hall-of-Fame women's head basketball coach watched Texas nail a 3-pointer at the buzzer to take a one-point halftime lead. Tonight, however, she would not be headed to the locker room to talk to her players.

This was Feb. 1, 2014, and this was Baylor's annual Family Night, a special occasion when players and parents took the court together at halftime. On this night during the intermission, Mulkey stood at center court with her starting senior small forward, who was also her daughter, Makenzie Robertson.

Robertson joked at one point that she was worried her mom wouldn't show. "She knew at that moment I was focused on what I wanted to show them in the locker room and say to them," Mulkey said.

An unwritten rule of college sports is that a recruit should never pick a school because of a coach. In this case, that rule was clearly broken. Robertson never seriously entertained the major college offers she received. Her dream was to play college ball for one coach only: her mother.

They managed to make it work, separating the disparate roles each brought to the relationship. "Anything she says to me on the court," Robertson said, "I never take personally because it's two different roles, being my mom and being my coach."

Mulkey admitted during the 2014 season that she had made one regrettable mistake about Makenzie's career at Baylor. Intent on showing an absence favoritism, she didn't give her daughter enough playing time before her senior season.

By the way, the Lady Bears whipped Texas 87-73.

Mamas often do what Kim Mulkey did on Family Night 2014: change their plans for the sake of a child. No mother in history, though, has faced a challenge to match that of Mary, whom God chose to be the mother of Jesus. Like mamas and their children throughout time, Mary experienced both joy and perplexity in her relationship with her son.

To the end, though, Mary stood by her boy. She followed him all the way to his execution, an act of love and bravery since Jesus was condemned as an enemy of the Roman Empire.

But just as mothers like Mary — and perhaps yours — would do just about anything for their children, so will God do anything out of love for his children. After all, that was God on the cross at the foot of which Mary stood, and he was dying for you, one of his children.

My mom's a very blunt person. She tells it like it is, it doesn't matter who you are. But she'd always give me credit if I did something good.
— Makenzie Robertson on playing for Kim Mulkey

**Mamas often sacrifice for their children,
but God, too, will do anything for his children,
including dying on a cross.**

HOLLYWOOD ENDING

Read Luke 24:1-12.

"Why do you look for the living among the dead? He is not here; he has risen!" (vv. 5, 6a)

Grant Teaff's last home game as Baylor's head football coach was a win, in large part because of something that happened even Hollywood wouldn't touch. Nobody would believe it.

In August 1992, the winningest coach in the school's football history announced the season would be his last. The team was a solid underdog for the season-ending Texas game on Nov. 21 in Floyd Casey Stadium.

On the team was senior defensive back Trooper Taylor, who finished as the school's all-time leader in kickoff returns and return yardage. Knee surgery sidelined him for the season; he had not even recovered to the point that he could work out.

Nevertheless, the week of the Texas game he came to Teaff with an astonishing request: He asked his coach to put him in for one play. "I want to play in your last game and my last game," he said Stunned, Teaff replied, "Trooper, we're playing the University of Texas." "Coach, please don't say no," Taylor urged. "Just tell me you'll think about it." Teaff said he would.

During the game, Taylor repeatedly asked his coach if he had thought about it, and his persistence finally wore Teaff down. He told a coach to put Taylor in for one play sometime in the last half.

The fired-up Bears led 21-20, but Texas sat at the Baylor 39 with two minutes left. The Horns went for the two yards they needed for the first down. A halfback hit the line and lunged toward the first down when "seemingly from out of nowhere," a defender stopped him four inches short. Baylor had the ball and the upset.

As Teaff sent the offense in to run out the clock, a green jersey jumped up in front of him and shouted, "I made the tackle! I made the tackle!" In an ending that even Hollywood would say was too hokey to believe, the player was Trooper Taylor.

The world tells us that happy endings are for fairy tales and the movies, that reality is Cinderella dying in childbirth and her prince getting killed in a peasant uprising. But that's just another of the world's lies.

The truth is that Jesus Christ has been producing very happy endings for almost two millennia. That's because in Jesus lies the power to change and to rescue a life no matter how desperate the situation. Jesus is the master at putting shattered lives back together, of healing broken hearts and broken relationships, of resurrecting lost dreams.

And as for living happily ever after – God really means it. The greatest Hollywood ending of them all was written on a Sunday morning centuries ago when Jesus left a tomb and death behind. With faith in Jesus, your life can have that same ending. You live with God in peace, joy, and love – forever. The End.

This is not up for discussion. Put Trooper Taylor in for one play.
— Grant Teaff to secondary coach Scott Smith

**Hollywood's happy endings are products
of imagination; the happy endings Jesus
produces are real and are yours for the asking.**

HOPE CHEST

Read Psalm 42.

"Put your hope in God, for I will yet praise him, my Savior and my God" (v. 5b).

The Art Briles era at Baylor didn't start out as Bear fans hoped it would. But what became known as "the play" offered a promise of real hope.

A new chapter of Baylor football began on Aug. 28, 2008, with Briles' first game as BU's head football coach. It was also the beginning of the era of Robert Griffin III, who didn't even start that night against Wake Forest. Briles decided to go with the more experienced Kirby Freeman, a senior transfer from Miami.

All the hopes for a grand start to a new age of BU football were crushed. Wake built an early 17-0 lead, and in the third quarter, the game was out of hand at 34-6, "which sent many of the fans to the exits early, something Baylor folks were all too familiar with."

Amid of that apparent hopelessness, however, there was "the play." Inserted into the game in the second quarter, Griffin swept to the left side and turned upfield right into the path of a Deacon defender. It looked like a simple four-yard run.

But Griffin suddenly hit the brakes and hopped backward a yard. The defender flew by him into the Baylor bench. Griffin then headed up the sideline for a 22-yard gain. That one play offered hope of a future filled with excitement the likes of which Baylor fans had not seen for a while.

BEARS

It also offered hope for the future in another way. At the game was a recruit named Ahmad Dixon, who wasn't seriously considering Baylor. Then came "the play." "I didn't think [Baylor] had players who could do things like that," he said. "When I saw that, I instantly changed my perception of Baylor." Two years later, Dixon became the highest-ranked recruit Baylor had ever signed.

Despite the loss that night, hope had sprung to life in Waco.

Only when a life has no hope does it become not worth the living. To hope is not merely to want something; that is desire or wishful thinking. Desire must be coupled with some degree of expectation to produce hope.

Therein lies the great problem. We may wish for a million dollars, relief from our diabetes, world peace, or a way to lose weight while stuffing ourselves with doughnuts and fried chicken. Our hopes, however, must be firmly grounded, or they will inevitably lead us to disappointment, shame, and disaster. In other words, false hopes ruin us.

One of the most basic issues of our lives, therefore, becomes discovering or locating that in which we can place our hope. Where can we find sure promises for a future that we can count on? Where can we place our hope with realistic expectations that we can live securely even though some of the promises we rely on are yet to be delivered?

In God. In God and God alone lies our hope.

The run was an exciting effort for a Baylor team in need of a lift.
— *Nick Eatman on the hope found in RGIII's 22-yard run vs. Wake*

God and his sustaining power are the source of the only meaningful hope possible in our lives.

DAY 66

THE SIMPLE LIFE

Read 1 John 1:5-10.

"If we confess our sins, he is faithful and just and will forgive us our sins and purify us from all unrighteousness" (v. 9).

His track record at Baylor proves conclusively that Art Briles can coach a quarterback. He has a basic formula: Keep it simple.

As Mark Schlabach of *ESPN* put it in 2013, "The Bears have been able to plug in one quarterback after another and not miss a beat on offense." The beat started, of course, with Robert Griffin III, who set the school record and won the Heisman Trophy in 2011 with 4,293 yards passing. He left and senior Nick Florence stepped up and broke Griffin's record in 2012 with 4,309 yards passing. He left and junior Bryce Petty stepped up and accounted for 82 touchdowns in 2013 and '14. The Bears won two Big 12 titles and led the country in yards per game and points.

The quarterbacks all ran Briles' fast-paced spread offense, and they ran it as simply as possible, so simply that they didn't even have a playbook to learn. Briles abandoned the use of a playbook long before he took over at Waco.

Instead, Briles and his coaches teach their QBs through repetition at practice and hours of watching video. "Kids play video games, so we show them the plays on video," Briles said. "Everything is on an iPad, and we label it and number them."

Briles also keeps game management simple for his quarterbacks by not asking them to do too much despite the rapid pace of Baylor's offense. The coaches minimize the pre-snap reads required of the quarterback. Often, it's the running backs or tight ends who read the defense and bark out the blocking schemes.

"We try to ease the load on the quarterbacks," Briles said. At Baylor that means, keeping it simple.

Perhaps the simple life in America was doomed by the arrival of the programmable VCR, itself rendered defunct by more sophisticated technology. Since then, we've been on what seems to be an inevitably downward spiral into ever more complicated lives. The once-simple telephone now does everything but walk the dog, and clothes dryers look like cockpits.

But we might do well in our own lives to mimic the simple formula Art Briles uses with his quarterbacks. That is, we should approach our lives with the keen awareness that success requires simplicity, a sticking to the basics: revere God, love our families, honor our country, do our best.

Theologians may make what God did in Jesus as complicated as quantum mechanics and the rules of dating in the 21st century, but God kept it simple for us: believe, trust, and obey. Believe in Jesus as the Son of God, trust that through him God makes possible our deliverance from our sins into Heaven, and obey God in the way he wants us to live.

That's the simple, true, and winning formula.

The less a quarterback has to think, the faster he can play.
— Art Briles on keeping it simple

Life is complicated, but God made it simple for us
when he showed up as Jesus.

THE JESUS WAY

Read Romans 13:8-14.

"The night is nearly over; the day is almost here. So let us put aside the deeds of darkness and put on the armor of light" (v. 12).

Mickey Sullivan had a way of coaching that was all his own. Whatever it was, it worked.

In 2014, Sullivan became the first-ever Baylor player or coach to be inducted into the National College Baseball Hall of Fame. As a senior at Baylor in 1954, he set the Southwest Conference record with a .519 batting average. Starting in 1974, Sullivan coached Baylor's baseball team for 21 seasons, compiling a 649-428-4 record. During his tenure, the Bears won three SWC titles and made it to the College World Series in 1977 and '78.

As writer Kevin Sherrington put it, "Baylor baseball under Sullivan was generally good and occasionally great but always entertaining." "We were a lot looser," was how pitcher Jonathan Perlman, a first-round draft pick in 1979 who made it to the major leagues, explained the Sullivan way.

For instance, Sullivan wasn't much for signs from his third-base coaching box. "If you were on first base," said Marty Crawford, a star second baseman in the '90s, "he might tilt his head toward second if he wanted you to steal. If you were on third, he'd turn his back to the catcher and give you the, 'Hey, c'mere' sign."

Sullivan made no apologies for being a player's coach. He not only took walk-ons, he started them. He preferred recruits who had played more than one sport in high school. He always let his hitters swing away. "He said he never saw a 2-0 pitch he didn't like," Crawford recalled.

The entertainment carried into the dugout. After the coach won his 600th game, the players presented him a pipe. In a later game, as he paced the dugout puffing away, "he suddenly lost his temper and then his prize," throwing it with a vehemence. The pipe "bounced off the floor, a wall and back to its owner, who calmly resumed puffing." "The dugout erupted," Crawford said.

Like Mickey Sullivan, you have a way of life that defines and describes you. You're a die-hard Baylor fan for starters. Maybe you're married with a family. A city guy or a small-town gal. You wear jeans or a suit to work every day. And then there's your faith.

For the Christian, following Jesus more than anything else defines for the world your way of life. It's basically simple in its concept even if it is downright daunting in its execution. You act toward others in a way that would not embarrass you were your day to be broadcast on Fox News. You think about others in a way that would not humiliate you should your thoughts be the plot line for a new CBS sitcom.

You make your actions and thoughts those of love: at all times, in all things, toward all people. It's the Jesus way of life, and it's the way to life forever with God.

I wasn't soft on my boys. I was just for them.
— Mickey Sullivan, explaining the way he coached

To live the Jesus way is to act with love at all times, in all things, and toward all people.

FOOD FOR THOUGHT

Read Genesis 9:1-7.

"Everything that lives and moves will be food for you. Just as I gave you the green plants, I now give you everything" (v. 3).

Grant Teaff was willing to do just about anything to help his team get ready for Texas — even eat a worm.

The Bears ended the 1978 football season on Nov. 25 at home against the ninth-ranked Longhorns. Seeking a way to pull off the upset, Teaff moved Mickey Elam, a backup running back, to quarterback and installed him as the starter. Elam wasn't a passer, which Texas didn't know, but he could run the option. "I believed the option would defeat Texas," Teaff said.

It would work, though, only if every player, as Teaff put it, did whatever it took to succeed. He told his team the story of the two ice fishermen who sat only three feet apart. One was successful, the other wasn't. When the unsuccessful fishermen sought the reason for the other's success, the latter put a worm in his mouth with the admonition, "You've got to keep the worms warm."

The Friday night before the game, a backup tackle asked Teaff if there were any way he could demonstrate to the team his point about being successful. The head coach figured he could.

The next day just before the Bears took the field, Teaff stepped on a bench and launched into a pep talk. He concluded by declaring, "There's not much we as coaches can do while you win the game, but there's one thing I will do. I'll keep the worms warm."

With that, he held a worm up and dropped it into the right corner of his mouth. The fired-up players tore onto the field while Teaff discreetly "popped my little friend into the trash." One of the surprised assistant coaches told him, "I'm glad you didn't call for volunteers."

The Bears ate Texas up 38-14.

Belly up to the buffet, boys and girls, for barbecue, sirloin steak, grilled chicken, and fried catfish. Hamburger joints, pizza parlors, and taco stands lurk on every corner; and we have a TV channel devoted exclusively to food. We love our chow, even if the menu doesn't usually include worms.

Food is one of God's really good ideas, but consider the complex divine plan that begins with a kernel and winds up with corn-on-the-cob slathered with butter and littered with salt. The creator of all life devised a downright fascinating and effective system in which living things are sustained and nourished physically through the sacrifice of other living things in a way similar to what Christ underwent to save us spiritually.

Whether it's fast food or home-cooked, practically everything we eat is a gift from God secured through a divine plan in which some plants and/or animals have given up their lives. Pausing to give thanks before we dive in seems the least we can do.

Personally, I don't think the worm had a thing to do with our victory.
— *Grant Teaff on his wriggly psychological ploy*

God created a system that nourishes us through the sacrifice of other living things; that's worth a thank-you.

NAME DROPPING

Read Exodus 3:13-20.

"God said to Moses, 'I AM WHO I AM. This is what you are to say to the Israelites: 'I AM has sent me to you''" (v. 14).

From the Stork to the White Freak, nicknames were a part of the 2013 Baylor football team.

Head coach Art Briles "makes [it] a habit to stamp a nickname on pretty much every player on his roster." Thus, All-American quarterback Bryce Petty was "Pettybone."

Kicker Aaron Jones, who set an NCAA record for career extra points, was dubbed "Stork." Unlike some of Briles' creations, this one caught on with the rest of the team. Jones even bought into it, using the Twitter nickname "StorkTheDork."

Backup quarterback Andrew Frerking got stuck with "White Freak," which may be better or worse than fellow backup Seth Russell's nickname, "Scotty." "I don't really know why," Petty said. "Maybe it's like a Scotty McCreery reference or something."

Running back Glasco Martin got hit with "Glass Pack," and All-American guard Cyril Richardson was "C-Note." Tevin Reese, who set the NCAA record for career touchdown receptions of 40+ yards, was "Sweet Feet." Junior receiver Levi Norwood probably answered very reluctantly when Briles called "Little No No."

One player on the squad, however, has come to be known by his nickname more than by his given name. He is Shock Linwood, who rushed for 881 yards in 2013 and 1,252 yards in 2014. Rashodrick Antoine Linwood was born during Shaquille O'Neal's rookie season in the NBA when the "Shaq Attack" was all the rage. Linwood's mom decided her son would be the "Shock Attack." During Linwood's childhood, he explained, people "got tired of saying the whole thing, so they just shortened it to Shock."

Nicknames such as "Shock" are usually not slapped haphazardly upon individuals but rather reflect widely held perceptions about the person named. Proper names can also have a particular physical or character trait associated with them.

Nowhere throughout the long march of history has this concept been more prevalent than in the Bible, where a name is not a mere label but is an expression of the essential nature of the named one. That is, a person's name reveals his or her character. This applies even to God; to know the name of God is to know God as he has chosen to reveal himself to us.

What does your name say about you? Honest, trustworthy, a seeker of the truth and a person of God? Or does the mention of your name cause your coworkers to whisper snide remarks, your neighbors to roll their eyes, or your friends to start making allowances for you?

Most importantly, what does your name say about you to God? He, too, knows you by name.

I don't really know where that came from.
— *Bryce Petty on his 'Pettybone' nickname*

Live so that your name evokes positive associations by people you know, by the public, and by God.

POP THE QUESTION

Read Matthew 16:13-17.

"'But what about you?' he asked. 'Who do you say I am?'" (v. 15)

For the pundits, the burning question was whether Baylor could slow down the national player of the year. As it turned out, that was the wrong question.

On Sunday, March 23, 2014, the sixth-seeded Baylor men took on the third-seeded Creighton Bluejays in the second round of the NCAA Tournament. The birds were led by Doug McDermott, the fifth leading scorer in NCAA history, and the player the basketball experts had a question about: Could Baylor handle him?

Their concerns were directed at the wrong team. The more pertinent question they should have been asking was whether Creighton could handle the juggernaut that the Baylor men had become. The correct answers to the two questions, respectively, were yes and no.

In a game that was no contest, the Bears blasted Creighton 85-55 to advance to the Sweet 16 for the third time in five seasons. The teams were tied at seven when Baylor ripped off a 12-0 run with four straight three-point shots. Royce O'Neale started the spree, and Kenny Chery and Brady Heslip followed up. Chery hit a second bomb, and with 13:03 to go in the first half, the game was essentially over. Baylor led 40-20 at halftime.

And that all-important question? "We got down defensively,

BEARS

and everybody did their assignment," declared head Bear Scott Drew. Indeed. McDermott wasn't a factor in the game, scoring only three points in the first half and not hitting a field goal the first seventeen minutes of the game. Baylor led 35-16 by then.

Clearly, the Bears had all the answers, no matter what the question was.

Life is an ongoing search for answers, and thus whether our life is lived richly or is wasted is largely determined by both the quality and the quantity of the answers we find. Life is indeed one question after another. What's for dinner? Can we afford a new car? What kind of team will Baylor have this season?

But we also continuously seek answers to questions at another, more crucial level. What will I do with my life? Why am I here? Why does God allow suffering and tragedy?

An aspect of wisdom is reconciling ourselves to and being comfortable with the fact that we will never know all of the answers. Equally wise is the realization that the answers to life's more momentous questions lie within us, not beyond us.

One question overrides all others, the one Jesus asked Peter: "Who do you say I am?" Peter gave the one and only correct answer: "You are the Son of the Living God." How you answer that question is really the only one that matters, since it decides not just how you spend your life but how you spend eternity.

The coaches prepared us and told us what to take away on defense, and we did a pretty good job of it.
— Brady Heslip on questions about handling Doug McDermott

**Only one question in life determines
your eternal fate: Who do you say Jesus is?**

THE OUTER LIMITS

Read Genesis 18:1-15.

"Is anything too hard for the Lord?" (v. 14a)

He was too small and too slow, the recruiters opined. Eddie Lackey simply ignored what they all said about him.

Despite an impressive high school resume, Lackey didn't draw any interest from major colleges. The coaches said that at 5-11, 220 lbs. he was too small to play linebacker and was not fast enough to play safety. They all passed on him.

He wound up at Division II Northwood University in Michigan. Why so far from his California home? "Northwood was the only place that would pay for my schooling," Lackey said. He had a solid season at safety but wasn't happy there, so he returned to California and Riverside Community College. Not giving up his dream of playing Division I football, he played linebacker at Riverside and had an outstanding season.

Meanwhile, in Waco, Baylor defensive coordinator Phil Bennett told intern Cody Alexander to get six guys on tape to evaluate. Bennett and linebackers coach Jim Gush then rated them, and they agreed: Eddie Lackey was the best of the bunch. They called him that night and asked if he had any interest in visiting Baylor. He did, of course, seeing as how he had nowhere else to go.

He was in Floyd Casey Stadium for the 2011 season finale, a 48-24 hammering of Texas. Lackey was so excited by the whole experience that he committed to Baylor before he left campus. He transferred to Baylor in the spring and quickly earned a starting linebacker spot. "They put me right in the lineup against the first team on the first day of spring practice," Lackey recounted.

This player who refused to be held back by what others saw as his limitations was an All-Big 12 first-team linebacker in both 2012 and 2013. He led the team in tackles as a senior in 2013.

You've probably never tried a whole bunch of things you've dreamed about doing at one time or another. Like starting your own business. Going back to school. Campaigning for elected office. Running a marathon.

But what holds you back? Perhaps you hesitate because you see only your limitations, both those you've imposed on yourself and those of which others constantly remind you. But maybe as Eddie Lackey did, it's time you ignored what everybody says. Maybe it's time to see yourself the way God does.

God sees you as you are and also as you can be. In God's eyes, your possibilities are limitless. The realization of those latent possibilities, however, depends upon your depending upon God for direction, guidance, and strength. While you may quail in the face of the challenge that lies before you, nothing is too hard for the Lord.

You can free yourself from that which blights your dreams by depending not on yourself but on God.

The recruiting game is all about finding the cookie cutter. [Eddie Lackey] was 5-11 and no one would give him a chance.
— High school football coach Coley Candaele

Pray like everything depends upon God;
work like everything depends upon you.

KEEPING THE PEACE

Read Hebrews 12:14-17.

"Make every effort to live in peace with all men and to be holy" (v. 14).

Baylor and Texas A&M had good reason to suspend athletic competition in 1926: At the football game, a riot broke out that left one cadet dead.

The second football game Baylor ever played — in 1899 — was against A&M. An immediate rivalry was born that only intensified when both schools joined as charter members of the Southwest Conference in 1914.

Fever may have been running high, but tempers were apparently under control at the 1926 game until halftime when, as Alan J. Lefever tells the story, some Baylor students drove a flatbed truck onto the field. On the truck – allegedly – were some Baylor coeds holding signs relating to recent wins over A&M.

The Aggies took exception to the way the coeds were dressed, though specifics of the attire are lost to history. The quite credible suggestion survives that some of the coeds weren't coeds at all but young men wearing women's clothes.

Intensely insulted, some Aggies charged the truck, and a full-fledged riot broke out. It ended only when the A&M band began playing the national anthem and the cadets stopped fighting and snapped to attention. According to Lefever, one Aggie was taken to a local hospital and died a few hours later of head trauma.

BEARS

An unverified postscript to the riot says that the cadets went back to College Station and loaded a cannon onto a railcar with the intent of returning to Waco and shelling the Baylor campus. The legend goes that some Texas Rangers intervened before the cadets could turn a riot into something much worse.

A few weeks later, the two school presidents met and decreed that athletic competition between the institutions would be suspended for four years. The teams did not meet again until 1931.

Perhaps you've never been in a brawl or a public brouhaha to match that of the Bears and the Aggies in 1926. But maybe you retaliated when you got one elbow too many in a pickup basketball game. Or maybe you and your spouse or your teenager get into it occasionally, shouting and saying cruel things. Or road rage may be a part of your life.

While we do seem to live in a more belligerent, confrontational society than ever before, fighting is still not the solution to a problem. Rather, it only escalates the whole confrontation, leaving wounded pride, intransigence, and simmering hatred in its wake. Actively seeking and making peace is the way to a solution that lasts and heals broken relationships and aching hearts.

Peacemaking is not as easy as fighting, but it is much more courageous and a lot less painful. It is also exactly what Jesus would do.

No matter what the other fellow does on the field, don't let him lure you into a fight. Uphold your dignity.
-- Legendary Alabama football coach Frank Thomas

Making peace instead of fighting takes courage and strength; it's also what Jesus would do.

THOSE THINGS

Read Luke 13:1-9.

"Or those eighteen who died when the tower in Siloam fell on them -- do you think they were more guilty than all the others living in Jerusalem? I tell you, no!" (vv 4, 5a)

T hose things" -- incidents that just seem to happen to an athlete -- include injuries. But going blind in one eye during a game?

Melissa Jones "will go down as one of the most beloved student-athletes in Baylor history." At the basketball awards ceremony in 2011 following Jones' senior season, head coach Kim Mulkey announced the 5-11 guard's No. 5 jersey had been retired and that the team's Hustle and Courage Award had been named for her. Jones rolled up some impressive statistics in Waco, but the Big 12 Conference 2011 Female Sportsperson of the Year garnered love and adoration for much more than her athletic ability.

On Feb. 27, 2011, against Oklahoma, Jones dived for a loose ball, and her head struck the court. During the next few minutes, the vision in her right eye faded from normal to fuzzy to complete blackness. She nevertheless played the rest of the game.

Her sight didn't return, but she missed only one game. Instead of complaining about the awful thing that had happened to her, she gave thanks to God for enabling her to play. "It was a special moment for me to see God's work," she said.

Wearing protective sunglasses on the court and playing with little more than total blindness in that right eye, Jones led Baylor in rebounding three times and in assists three times over the last eight games of the season. She was named to the Big 12 and the NCAA Regional all-tournament teams.

Because of her work ethic and her faith, Melissa Jones didn't let the injury stop her even after she graduated. In 2012, she said of her limited vision, "People think I'm winking at them when I try to focus. It's part of my life now and I have to adapt to it."

You've probably had a few of "those things" in your own life: bad breaks that occur without regard to justice, morality, or fair play. You wonder if everything in life is random with events determined by a chance roll of some cosmic dice. Is there really somebody scripting all this with logic and purpose?

Yes, there is; God is the author of everything.

We know how it all began; we even know how it all will end. It's in God's book. The part we play in God's kingdom, though, is in the middle, which is still being revealed to us. The simple truth is that God's ways are different from ours. After all, he's God and we are not. That's why we don't have any idea what's coming our way, and why "those things" — such as a sudden injury — catch us by surprise and dismay us when they do occur.

What God asks of us is that we trust him. As the one – and the only one – in charge, he knows everything will be all right for those who follow Jesus.

MJ didn't view [her blindness] as a roadblock, but as a speed bump.
— Guard Lindsay Palmer, teammate of Melissa Jones

Life confounds us because, while we know the end and the beginning of God's great story, we are part of the middle, which God is still writing.

HEART AND SOUL

Read Romans 12:1-2.

"Therefore, I urge you, brothers, in view of God's mercy, to offer your bodies as living sacrifices, holy and pleasing to God – this is your spiritual act of worship" (v. 1).

Following the 2009 season, Baylor fans learned of Art Briles' total commitment to the Bears when he passed on what could well have been termed his "dream job."

In the wake of what was deemed to be the mishandling of a player's injury, Texas Tech fired head coach Mike Leach, thus vacating a job that was certainly tempting to Briles. Not only had he graduated from Tech, but so had his wife. He had grown up in Rule in West Texas as a fan of the Red Raiders. If the Tech job wasn't the head Bear's dream job, it "was way more attractive to Briles than people realized."

Texas Tech officials immediately looked toward Waco. True, Briles' first two seasons at Baylor, both years with 4-8 records, didn't exactly raise any eyebrows, and the impatient coach wasn't very pleased with the eight wins himself.

The progress, however, was evident to anyone who bothered to look, and Tech officials did just that. Many of them knew the Baylor head coach personally, and the Red Raiders had managed to escape the Bears by only a touchdown both seasons.

Members of the Tech athletic department thus contacted Briles unofficially. He "was told by enough people — and [by] the right people — that he could have the job if he so desired."

As Briles "tossed and turned for about four nights," he wondered if Tech were not indeed a better fit for him, if the fan support at Baylor would ever be strong enough to fill the stadium, if he wouldn't win more games in Lubbock than he could in Waco.

In the end, though, Briles' commitment to Baylor and to Robert Griffin III won out. He just wasn't ready to give up on either the school or his special quarterback.

When you stood in a church and recited your wedding vows, did you make a decision that you could walk away from when things got tough or did you make a lifelong commitment? Is your job just a way to get a paycheck, or are you committed to it?

Commitment seems almost a dirty word in our society these days, a synonym for chains, an antonym for freedom. Perhaps this is why so many people are afraid of Jesus: Jesus demands commitment. To speak of offering yourself as "a living sacrifice" is not to speak blithely of making a decision but of heart-body-mind-and-soul commitment.

But commitment actually means "purpose and meaning," especially when you're talking about your life. Commitment makes life worthwhile. Anyway, in insisting upon commitment, Jesus isn't asking anything from you that he hasn't already given to you himself. His commitment to you was so deep that he died for you.

[Art Briles] was fully invested in Baylor.
— *Nick Eatman on the decision not to take the Tech job*

Commitment to Jesus lends meaning to your life, releasing you to move forward with purpose.

FATHERS AND SONS

Read Luke 3:1-22.

"And a voice came from heaven: 'You are my Son, whom I love; with you I am well pleased'" (v. 22).

From his goal of attending medical school to his love for the Texas Longhorns (That's right: Texas!), Stefan Huber has always been influenced by his father. Once he got to Baylor, though, the son did the influencing.

Since his dad, a family physician, played for the Longhorns in the 1970s, Stefan grew up in a Hook 'Em Horns household. Stefan dreamed of following in his dad's footsteps, both on the football field and in his profession.

That football dream ended one afternoon when Texas called and told the all-state offensive lineman that they had all the big bodies they needed. Texas might not have wanted Stefan, but Art Briles sure did.

When the Baylor head coach saw the family's Longhorn room, Dr. Huber told him, "'Coach Briles, I will make a deal with you. Each time we beat UT we have to switch something from orange to green in this room.' The first thing my wife did was redo the pool table with a Baylor logo."

The road in Waco wasn't an easy one to travel, though, for Stefan. He was redshirted in 2009 and then missed most of the 2010 and 2011 seasons because of injuries. He was a back-up in 2012. He didn't give up, however. He relied on the lessons about perseverance his father had taught him and on his faith. "If I didn't get injured, I wouldn't know how to work so hard in the dark to get ready for the light," he said.

In 2013, Stefan was the starting center for the Big 12 champions and earned All-Big 12 honorable mention honors. All the while, his dad, influenced by his son, proudly wore Baylor green "because that is where my son goes."

Contemporary American society largely belittles and marginalizes fathers and their influence upon their sons. Men are perceived as necessary to effect pregnancy; after that, they can leave and everybody's better off.

But we need look in only two places to appreciate the enormity of that misconception: our jails – packed with males who lacked the influence of fathers in their lives as they grew up -- and the Bible. God – being God – could have chosen any relationship he desired between Jesus and himself, including society's approach of irrelevancy.

Instead, the most important relationship in all of history was that of father-son. God obviously believes a close, loving relationship between fathers and sons, such as that of Stefan Huber and his dad, is crucial. For men and women to espouse otherwise or for men to walk blithely and carelessly out of their children's lives constitutes disobedience to the divine will.

Simply put, God loves fathers. After all, he is one.

Dad talked with me a lot and wanted me to push myself to be better.
— Stefan Huber

A model for the father-child relationship is found in that of Jesus the Son with God the Father.

THE INTERVIEW

Read Romans 14:1-12.

"We will all stand before God's judgment seat. . . . So then, each of us will give an account of himself to God" (*vv. 10, 12*).

Kendall Wright worked so hard to improve his pass-catching skills that he became the greatest receiver in Baylor history. At the same time, he had to work to improve his interviewing skills.

When Wright arrived in Waco in 2008 as a freshman, he didn't have a whole lot to say. He was comfortable around his teammates, but when reporters showed up, they had a hard time squeezing even a few words out of the gifted receiver.

Once, All-American tackle Jason Smith noticed a frustrated reporter struggling to interview Wright. Smith just shook his head and strode over to the pair. "Man, you've got to give him more than that," Smith told the rookie.

He then said he would pretend to be the receiver and told the reporter to ask him a question. The newsman obliged, asking, "What have you been working on all summer to improve as a receiver?" "Catching," Smith deadpanned.

The story always made Wright laugh when he recounted it. However, "[Baylor public relations] wouldn't let me bypass doing interviews, so I had to get used to it," he said. He took two interviewing classes and a public speaking course to improve. He also watched Smith and Robert Griffin III to pick up some pointers.

Wright had plenty of chances to "get used to it." He eventually became quite comfortable with the media though he never was the type of player who sought publicity. He finished in 2011 as a first-team All-America who set or tied sixteen school records, including career receptions, yardage, and touchdowns.

While you may not spend a lot of time being interviewed by reporters as Kendall Wright did, you nevertheless are probably quite familiar with a question-and-answer session of a different kind: the job interview.

You've experienced the stress, the anxiety, the helpless feeling that's part of any interview. You tried to appear calm and relaxed while struggling to come up with reasonably original answers to banal questions and to hide your considered opinion that the interviewer was a total geek. You told yourself that if they turned you down, it was their loss.

You won't be so indifferent or nonchalant, though, about your last interview: the one with God. A day will come when we will all stand before God to account for ourselves. It is to God and God alone – not our friends, not our parents, not society in general – that we must give a final and complete account.

In that final interview session, all eternity will be at stake and a resume of good deeds and sterling accomplishments won't help. What you will need is a reliable, surefire character reference you can call on. One — and only one — is available: Jesus Christ.

I'm in an advanced interviewing class now, and I think it's helped.
— Kendall Wright on improving his interviewing skills

You will have one last interview – with God – and you want Jesus with you as a character witness.

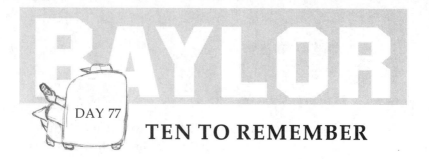

TEN TO REMEMBER

Read Exodus 20:1-17.

*"God spoke all these words: 'I am the Lord your God . . . .
You shall have no other gods before me'" (vv. 1, 3).*

The Baylor Bears are amidst one of the great program turn-arounds in college football history." So declared *ESPN*'s Jake Trotter, who then proceeded in Feb. 2015 to list the ten reasons why Baylor "became a [football] powerhouse."

First was the hiring of Art Briles in 2007 as the head football coach. Second was the signing of Robert Griffin III, who came along with Briles. The third factor Trotter listed was the school's surviving the turmoil of conference realignment and remaining in a Power Five Conference.

Fourth was the building of McLane Stadium. The "Jewel on the Brazos" has not only increased season-ticket sales but has elevated Baylor in the eyes of recruits. Trotter's fifth reason for Baylor's emergence is the success with the wide receivers. Kendall Wright, Terrance Williams, Tevin Reese, Corey Coleman, and KD Cannon have all allowed Baylor to lay claim to being Wide Receiver U for the way they have produced on the field.

Sixth is the coaching staff's ability to find hidden gems. For instance, running back Shock Linwood, All-Big 12 in 2104, had only one offer from a school in a Power Five Conference. The AP's Defensive Newcomer of the Year in 2014, Taylor Young, made only one other visit than to Baylor: Louisiana Monroe.

Trotter's seventh reason for Baylor's success is the hiring of defensive coordinator Phil Bennett. Eighth is bringing Lache Seastrunk home. He led the conference in rushing in 2013 and fueled the Bears' drive to the league championship.

Jazzing up the uniforms, which established a cutting-edge identity for the program, was Trotter's ninth reason for success. Tenth is the sensational job Baylor has done under Briles in developing quarterbacks, from Griffin to Nick Florence to Bryce Petty.

Like Jake Trotter's list of ten reasons for Baylor's turnaround, you've got your list and you're ready to go: a gallon of paint and a water hose from the hardware store; chips, peanuts, and sodas from the grocery store for watching tonight's football game with your buddies. Your list helps you remember.

God also made a list once of things he wanted you to remember; it's called the Ten Commandments. Just as your list reminds you to do something, so does God's list remind you of how you are to act in your dealings with other people and with him. A life dedicated to Jesus is a life devoted to relationships, and God's list emphasizes that the social life and the spiritual life of the faithful cannot be sundered.

God's relationship to you is one of unceasing, unqualified love, and you are to mirror that divine love in your relationships with others. In case you forget, you have a list.

Society today treats the Ten Commandments as if they were the ten suggestions. Never compromise on right or wrong.
— *College baseball coach Gordie Gillespie*

God's list is a set of instructions on how you are to conduct yourself with other people and with him.

UNSTOPPABLE!

Read Acts 5:29-42.

*"If it is from God, you will not be able to stop these men;
you will only find yourselves fighting against God" (v.
39).*

Once Odyssey Sims decided it was time for California to go
home, she and her Lady Bear teammates were unstoppable.

On March 24, 2014, in the second round of the NCAA Tournament, the 30-4 Baylor women found themselves in a bear brawl
with the 22-9 Golden Bears. Sims, the team's senior All-American
star, got into foul trouble early on, which sent her to the bench for
the last seven minutes of the first half. The two teams then traded
baskets until the break. Only when Cal missed three shots right
before the buzzer were the Lady Bears able to jog into the locker
room with a 34-33 lead.

Sims hit a pair of free throws and took a defensive rebound the
length of the floor for a layup that propelled Baylor into a 40-33
lead with 16:56 to play. But the Golden Bears refused to go away,
rallying to tie the game at 44.

About then, Sims decided it was time to settle this thing once
and for all, and "there was nothing the Golden Bears could do to
stop her." She scored 11 of her game-high 27 points during a 13-2
Baylor run capped by a 3-pointer from NBA range.

Baylor led 66-52 with 4:31 to go, and the Golden Bears were on
their way to a 75-56 loss. The Lady Bears, on the other hand, were

BEARS

on the way to their sixth straight Sweet 16.

Sims was unstoppable for much of her time at Baylor. A pair of national awards bookended the 5-8 guard's career: the National Freshman of the Year award in 2011 and the Nancy Lieberman Award as the nation's top point guard in 2014. She was a three-time All-America. Unstoppable offensively, she scored 1,054 points her senior season, only the second women's player in Division I history to score more than 1,000 points in a single season.

With stars such as Odyssey Sims on hand, the Lady Bears have been virtually unstoppable for the last decade or so. Isn't that the way we would like our life to unfold? One success after another in our career, our family, our investments – whatever we tackle. Unstoppable. The reality is, though, that life isn't like that at all. At some point, we all run into setbacks that stop us dead in our tracks. Everyone does – except God.

For almost two thousand years, the enemies of God have tried to stop Jesus and his people. They killed Jesus; they have persecuted and martyred his followers. Today, heretics, infidels, and pagans — many of them in America — are more active in their war on Christianity than at any other time in history.

And yet, the Kingdom of God advances, unstoppable despite all opposition. Pursuing God's purposes in our lives puts us on a team bound for glory. Fighting against God gets his enemies nowhere. Except Hell.

I scored when I needed to, and I passed the ball when I needed to.
— Odyssey Sims on her unstoppable last half vs. Cal

**God's kingdom and purposes are unstoppable
no matter what his enemies try.**

MYSTERIOUS WAYS

Read Romans 11:25-36.

"O the depth of the riches and wisdom and knowledge of God! How unsearchable are his judgments and how inscrutable his ways!" (v. 33 NRSV)

Perhaps the most enigmatic team Baylor has ever fielded was the 1966 squad, which beat two top-ten teams but won only five games.

The Bears opened the season on Sept. 10 on national television against seventh-ranked Syracuse. The Orangemen were loaded with Floyd Little and Larry Csonka in the backfield. The Bears had finished 5-5 in 1965.

Before the largest crowd ever to see a home opener, the Bears stunned Syracuse 35-12. Quarterback Terry Southall, coming off a knee injury, tied a school record by throwing four touchdown passes before sitting out the fourth quarter.

With the upset, the Bears jumped to No. 10 in the AP poll. And promptly revealed what a mystery they were by losing their next game to Colorado 13-7. They followed that up by squeezing past a Washington State team that won only three games, 20-14.

So the verdict was out: This team really wasn't that good and would get crushed on Oct. 8 by the undefeated and fifth-ranked Arkansas Razorbacks, the defending national champions. Led by Jerry Haney, Billy Burk, Greg Pipes, and David Anderson, the Bears shut Arkansas down completely. In what was called the

BEARS

"Golden Bears' . . . finest hour," they upset the Hogs 7-0.

Thinking he had this team all figured out, Arkansas head coach Frank Broyles declared, "People are going to have a hard time beating Baylor." Not at all. This mystery of a team lost its next three games, including TCU, which won only twice all season.

The good Lord sure works in mysterious ways. It's an old saying among people of faith, an acknowledgment of the limits of our understanding of God.

Such a realization serves to make God even more tantalizing because human nature loves a good mystery. We relish the challenge of uncovering what somebody else wants to hide. We are intrigued by a whodunit such as *NCIS*, a rousing round of Clue, or reruns of *Matlock* or *Perry Mason*.

Some mysteries are simply beyond our knowing, however. Events in our lives that are in actuality the mysterious ways of God remain so to us because we can't see the divine machinations. We can see only the results, appreciate that God was behind it all, and give him thanks and praise.

God has revealed much about himself, especially through Jesus, but still much remains unknowable. Why does he tolerate the existence of evil? What does he really look like? Why is he so fond of bugs? What was the inspiration for chocolate?

We know for sure, though, that God is love, and so we proceed with life, assured that one day all mysteries will be revealed.

Inconsistency led Baylor to finish 5-5 for the season.
— Writer Luke Blount, trying to explain the mystery of the 1966 team

**God keeps much about himself shrouded in
mystery, but one day we will see and understand.**

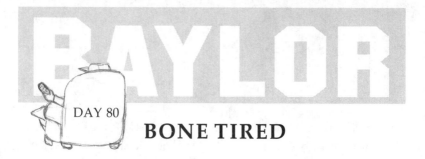

BONE TIRED

Read Matthew 11:27-30.

"Come to me, all you who are weary and burdened, and I will give you rest" (v. 11).

Beat-up, rain-soaked, and worn out. They were a sorry looking bunch, those Baylor offensive linemen. But they had just finished doing something downright magnificent.

The Bears thumped Oklahoma State 49-28 on Nov. 22, 2014, to lift their record to 9-1. On "a dreary and rainy night along the banks of the Brazos River," Baylor took advantage of the weather.

In the first quarter, the Bears ground out their longest offensive drive in two years. By Baylor standards, the drive was clearly "ugly." None of the plays were particularly memorable. When it was all over and done with, though, the drive was one for the offensive linemen to cherish.

The Baylor offense ran nineteen plays and was on the field for ten minutes. Fifteen rushes and only four pass attempts made up the drive. Thanks to four penalties, the Bears had to travel 94 yards on what amounted to a 79-yard drive. Four second and longs. Four third downs. One fourth down. Ten of the fifteen rushes gained fewer than four yards. Still, the Bears kept the sticks and the clock moving.

Running back Devin Chafin had seven of his 21 carries during the drive. He ended it with a 2-yard score. "As running backs, we favor the rainy, muddy, grimy games," he said.

BEARS

And then there were the linemen: tackles Spencer Drango and Troy Baker, guards Blake Muir and Jarrell Broxton, and center Kyle Fuller. When the drive ended, they collapsed onto a sideline bench. "They were just gasping," head coach Art Briles said. "I thought, 'What's the deal?'" So Briles used his headset to ask an assistant coach how many plays they had run. When the answer came, his reaction was, "Wow!"

Like offensive linemen in a long drive, the everyday struggles and burdens of life beat us down. They may be enormous; they may be trivial with a cumulative effect, but they tire us out. We even have a name for our exhaustion: chronic fatigue syndrome.

Doctors don't help too much. Sleeping pills can zonk us out; muscle relaxers can dull the weariness. Other than that, it's drag on as usual until we can collapse exhaustedly into bed.

Then along comes Jesus, as usual offering hope and relief for what ails us, though in a totally unexpected way. He says take my yoke. Whoa, there! Isn't a yoke a device for work? Exactly.

The mistake we all too often make lies in trying to do it alone. We rely on ourselves instead of Jesus. If we yoke ourselves to our Lord, the unimaginable, limitless power of almighty God is at our disposal to do the heavy lifting for us.

God's strong shoulders and broad back can handle any burdens we can give him. We just have to let them go.

That was, uh . . . um, tiring.
  — Left tackle Spencer Drango on the 19-play drive vs. OSU

**Tired and weary are a way of life
only when we fail to accept Jesus' invitation
to swap our burden for his.**

RED-FACED

Read John 2:1-11.

Jesus' mother said to him, 'They have no more wine.'" (v. 3)

The Bears were on the verge of a collapse of epic and embarrassing proportions. Then their All-American catcher bailed them out.

On its way to the 2011 NCAA Tournament, Baylor's baseball team met Texas Tech on Saturday, March 19. For eight innings, the game bordered on the boring as the Bears dominated.

A hint that the game might turn out to be pretty wacky before it was all over came in the Baylor second. On three separate at-bats, the Bears scored four runs on only one hit, and even that one was unusual. Sophomore third-baseman Jake Miller, for instance, walked and came all the way around on a pair of errors. Two batters later, senior outfielder Chris Slater drilled a home run, the first inside-the-park job by a Bear in five years.

All that excitement helped Baylor jump out to an 11-2 lead after four innings, and the Bears held it, ahead quite safely at 13-4 as the ninth inning started. That's when everything fell apart.

Incredibly, Texas Tech scored nine runs with six of the runs crossing after two were out. When Baylor finally recorded its twenty-seventh out, the score – quite embarrassingly – was tied. That embarrassment continued into the bottom of the ninth when the first two batters recorded outs.

Then, however, the Bears showed they were "shellshocked but

not felled." First baseman Max Muncy took one for the team – a pitch right side his helmet. Joey Hainsfurther singled, and that brought junior catcher Josh Ludy to the plate. As a senior in 2012, he would be named a first-team All-America after hitting .362 with 16 home runs. Ludy came through, dropping a two-strike pitch into shallow right field. Muncy scored and the Bears had avoided an embarrassing defeat.

A sports team collapses for an epic loss or gets the daylights beat out of it. A wedding party runs out of food and/or drink. We say something unbelievably dumb or trip over our own feet with everybody watching. Man, that's embarrassing! We've all been there, done that.

Many of us, though, allow embarrassment to encroach onto our faith life where it has no business. We're so embarrassed to be a Christian that we won't claim the name of Christ in public. Many preachers are so embarrassed by the truth of the Gospel that they soft-peddle a twisted, convenient, and easy message from the pulpit. We cringe when friends talk openly, without embarrassment, about their faith. Defenders of the faith are even called apologetics as if we must apologize for what we believe.

But here's the awful flip side. Our embarrassment means that we are an embarrassment to Jesus. That doesn't serve just to embarrass us; it condemns us.

It's a good thing we stopped them at 13; otherwise it would have been a tough run there at the end.
    — Max Muncy on avoiding an embarrassing loss to Texas Tech

**If Jesus embarrasses us, then we are an
embarrassment to him; thus, we stand condemned.**

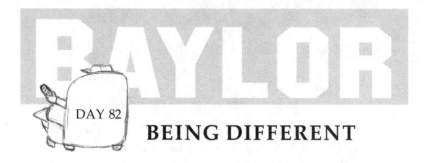

BEING DIFFERENT

Read Daniel 3.

*"We want you to know, O king, that we will not serve
your gods or worship the image of gold you have set up"*
(v. 18).

New head coach Grant Teaff was searching for a way to put
some pride back into a Baylor football program that had fallen
onto some hard times. He found it in "The Difference at Baylor."

The seniors Teaff inherited for the 1972 season — his first at
Baylor — had won only three games in three years. The facilities
were in bad shape also. So one of the first tasks the new coaches
took on was to change the attitude, to instill some pride, confidence, and cockiness in the players that would spread to the
student body and to the fans. One of the more successful of their
efforts was instigated by several students.

The Monday morning before the Texas A&M game of Oct.
28, 1972, some students came to Teaff's office with a proposal:
"Because you are a Christian coach at a Christian university, we
would like to hand out something at the game that would serve
as a testimony regarding the difference at Baylor." They wanted
to distribute a pamphlet emblazoned "The Difference at Baylor."
The inside bore Teaff's quote, "The greatest victory is not on the
football field, but through a personal relationship with Jesus
Christ." The plan of salvation was printed with the quote.

Teaff approved the idea, but one of the assistant coaches pro-

BEARS

tested that the message being sent was that winning the game was not important. The head coach replied, "You misinterpreted the message, and we will find a way to win."

They did indeed. A late field goal struck an upright, ricocheted straight up, came down on the crossbar, bounced up again, and fell gently into the end zone. It made the difference in the game; the Bears had a 15-13 win.

While we live in a secular society that constantly pressures us to conform to its principles and values, we serve a risen Christ who calls us to be different. Therein lies the great conflict of the Christian life in contemporary America.

But how many of us really consider that even in our secular society we struggle to conform? We are all geeks in a sense. We can never truly conform because we were not created by God to live in such a sin-filled world in the first place. Thus, when Christ calls us to be different by following and espousing Christian beliefs, principles, and practices, he is summoning us to the lifestyle we were born for.

The most important step in being different for Jesus is realizing and admitting what we really are: We are children of God; we are Christians. Only secondarily are we citizens of a secular world. That world both scorns and disdains us for being different; Jesus both praises and loves us for it.

I heard from many former students, fans, and even some Aggies who were touched by [the] effort to show there was a 'Difference at Baylor.'
— Grant Teaff

The lifestyle Jesus calls us to is different from that of the world, but it is the way we were born to live.

ONE-MAN ARMY

Read Revelation 19:11-21.

"The rest of them were killed by the sword that came out of the mouth of the rider on the horse" (v. 21).

Baylor had a football player who once volunteered to play the other team by himself if it would run only between the tackles.

Before the 1910 game, the Baylor and Texas coaches disagreed mightily about which of the officials should serve as referee and run the game. Texas won out and chose an official with whom the Longhorn coach had some ties.

As the game wore on, the suspect ref — at least from the Baylor perspective — "was giving Texas all the better of it in his calls." Once, he got in the way of a Baylor player who had broken open for an apparent touchdown, enabling Texas to catch him from behind at the Longhorn 18.

Late in the game with the score tied at 6, Baylor end Riley Hefley picked up a fumble and started to run with it. The referee stopped him, declaring the play to be dead because the ball had struck him, the ref. Two of the other three officials disagreed, but the referee refused to change his decision. At this point, Baylor captain/coach Ralph Glaze refused to let his team continue and took his players off the field, thereby ending the game.

Texas listed the game as a 1-0 victory in its record book while for years, Baylor insisted the game ended in a 6-6 tie.

One Baylor player, however, had no interest in leaving. E.T.

BEARS

"Bull" Adams, described as "a mighty lineman" who went on to be a Rhodes Scholar, had scored Baylor's touchdown by running 20 yards with a fumble recovery. When Glaze decided to leave the field with his team, Adams wouldn't go.

Instead, he declared he would act as a one-man army. He challenged the Longhorns to run the rest of their plays only between the tackles. If they would do so, he said, he would take them on by himself.

Texas declined Adams' bold, flamboyant request and left.

A similar but more dire and serious situation will occur when Christ returns. He will not come back to us as the meek lamb led unprotestingly to slaughter on the cross. Instead, he will be a one-man army, a rider on a white horse who will destroy those forces responsible for disorder and chaos in God's world.

This image of our Jesus as a warrior may well shock and discomfort us; it should also excite and thrill us. It reminds us vividly that God will unleash his awesome power to effect justice and righteousness in a world that persecutes his people and slanders his name. It should also lend us a sense of urgency because the time will pass when decisions for Christ can still be made.

For now, Jesus has an army at his disposal in the billions of Christians around the world. We are Christian soldiers; we have a world to conquer for our Lord – before he returns as a one-man army to finish the job.

The raging and defiant [E.T.] Adams initially refused to go.
— 'Program History' on Baylor's would-be one-man army vs. Texas

**Jesus will return as a one-man army to conquer
the forces of evil; for now, we are his army.**

CALLING IT QUITS

Read Numbers 13:25-14:4.

"The men who had gone up with him said, 'We can't attack those people; they are stronger than we are'" (v. 13:31).

Players quit football for any number of reasons. How many of them, however, have their gridiron careers sidelined — as Cyril Richardson's almost was — by the weather?

As a senior at Baylor in 2013, Richardson was a first-team All-American guard. He is the only two-time Offensive Lineman of the Year in Big 12 history. All this success came after he had decided to quit football before he ever really got started.

During Richardson's freshman year of high school in New Orleans, Hurricane Katrina hit. Thus began a two-year stretch in which Richardson and his family moved to an aunt's house in Baton Rouge, to two different trailer parks, to his sister's house in North Texas, and finally to Fort Worth.

All the moves left Richardson's football career in shambles. He was behind academically. Also, he hadn't decided to play football until the summer before his freshman year — the one that was wiped out by the hurricane. He then lost his sophomore year of football as the family moved from place to place.

That's when Richardson decided to quit. That's also when his brother stepped up. "My brother pushed me back into it and I'm glad he did," Richardson said. Finally, as a junior, he made it onto the field — only to lose half the season to academic ineligibility brought on by all the moves.

Those academic problems led him to Baylor. In summer school to catch up, he missed a TCU camp he wanted to attend. He had caught up on his work, though, by the time of a Baylor camp, so he went. Offensive line coach Randy Clements offered him a scholarship at the end of the day and he accepted.

Baylor had a future All-America on its hands who came close to quitting football because of problems caused by the weather.

Remember that time you quit a high-school sports team? Or that night you bailed out of a relationship? Walked away from a job with the goals unachieved? Sometimes quitting is the most sensible way to minimize your losses, so you may well at times in your life give up on something or someone.

In your relationship with God, however, you should remember the people of Israel, who quit when the Promised Land was theirs for the taking. They forgot one fact of life you never should: God never gives up on you.

That means you should never, ever give up on God. No matter how tired or discouraged you get, no matter that it seems your prayers aren't getting through to God, no matter what — quitting on God is not an option.

He is preparing a blessing for you, and in his time, he will bring it to fruition -- if you don't quit on him.

My brother saw something in me that I didn't realize.
— Cyril Richardson on his brother's urging him not to quit football

Whatever else you give up on in your life, don't give up on God; he will never ever give up on you.

NO EXCUSE

Read Luke 9:57-62.

"Another said, 'I will follow you, Lord; but first let me go back and say good-by to my family'" (v. 61).

Isaiah Austin would not even consider any excuse that kept him from playing basketball — not even being blind in one eye.

When he was 12, Austin was struck in the right eye by a baseball thrown his way when he wasn't looking. Doctors found no vision problems, but did detect that his retina was loose. "They said that it did have a chance of tearing or ripping," Austin said.

They were right. When Austin was in the eighth grade and already a towering 6-7, he pulled off a routine pregame dunk. He suddenly realized he could see only red out of his right eye. His retina was detached.

Multiple surgeries followed in attempts to save Austin's vision, but they were unsuccessful. He had some blurred vision for a time, but eventually was totally blind in the eye.

Austin's mother told him, "You can touch lives or you can be a quitter." He chose not to quit and went back to work on his basketball game. He had to change the way he played, describing his new style as keeping his head on a swivel in the paint to see as much of the court as possible.

Austin developed into a top national recruit and committed to Baylor, entering school in 2012. He didn't tell Bear head coach Scott Drew about his blindness until after he committed. He also

BEARS

practiced for several weeks with his new teammates before he let them in on the secret of his prosthetic eye.

In January of 2014, Austin shared his story nationally on *ESPN*. "I want to be somebody that some kid looks up to saying if he can do it, then I can do it," Austin explained.

In other words, Isaiah Austin made no excuses. He proved that he could indeed do it, being named Honorable Mention All-Big 12 and to the coaches' All-Defense Team as a sophomore in 2014. He opted for the NBA but a genetic condition ended his career.

Has some of your most creative thinking involved excuses for not going in to work? Have you discovered that an unintended benefit of computers is that you can always blame them for the destruction of all your hard work? Don't you manage to stammer or stutter some justification when a state trooper pulls you over? We're usually pretty good at making excuses to cover our failures or to get out of something we don't particularly want to do.

That holds true for our faith life also. The Bible is too hard to understand so I won't read it; the weather's too pretty to be shut up in church; praying in public is embarrassing and I'm not very good at it anyway. The plain truth is, though, that whatever excuses we make for not following Jesus wholeheartedly are not good enough.

Jesus made no excuses to avoid dying for us; we should offer none to avoid living for him.

You can make it your excuse, or you can make it your story.
— *Isaiah Austin's mother to her son on his blindness*

**Try though we might, no excuses can justify
our failure to follow Jesus wholeheartedly.**

HOW DISAPPOINTING!

Read Ezra 3.

"Many of the older priests and Levites and family heads, who had seen the former temple, wept aloud when they saw the foundation of this temple being laid, while many others shouted for joy" (v. 12).

For Raynor Campbell, 2009 was the most disappointing year of his young life. Still, he would never take it back because of what he learned and gained.

Campbell began playing baseball when he was 6 in Norway of all places. After he set his high-school record for highest batting average (.495), the colleges came calling. He chose Baylor because "it felt like home," including its Christian environment.

The transition to the college game came easy for him. Campbell hit .321 as a freshman in 2007 and was a Freshman All-America and the Big 12 Freshman of the Year. A thumb injury cost him some games his sophomore season, but he still hit .311 and led the Bears in league play with a .354 average.

Then came 2009. The hits stopped coming and shortstop got tougher. Campbell bounced around between positions, and in desperation switched to a wooden bat in an attempt to replicate the success he had enjoyed in the Cape Cod Summer League. He was dropped to the bottom of the lineup and hit only .243 for the season. "It was very frustrating," Campbell admitted.

So why wouldn't he erase the year if he could? "It taught me so much," Campbell said. "I became a better Christian and I became a better ballplayer. . . . It taught me a lot of things about myself."

Campbell enjoyed "a righteous rebirth" in 2010. He hit .335, second on the team, and earned Honorable Mention All-Big 12 plaudits. On March 10, he was named the National Player of the Week. He was drafted by the San Francisco Giants.

As Raynor Campbell did, we know disappointment. Friends lie to us or betray us; we lose our jobs; emotional distance grows between us and our children; the Bears lose; our dreams shatter.

Disappointment occurs when something or somebody fails to meet the expectations we have for them. Since people are people and can't do anything about that, they inevitably will disappoint us. What is absolutely crucial to our day-to-day living, therefore, is not avoiding disappointment but handling it.

One approach is to act as the old people of Israel did at the dedication of the temple. Instead of joyously celebrating the construction of a new place of worship, they wailed and moaned about the lost glories of the old one. They chose disappointment over lost glories rather than the wonders of the present reality.

Disappointment can paralyze us all, but only if we lose sight of an immutable truth: Our lives may not always be what we wish they were, but God is still good to us.

There's nothing disappointing about that.

I found Christ on a better level than where I was before that. I wouldn't trade that year for anything.
— Raynor Campbell on his 'disappointing' 2009 season

Even in disappointing times, we can be confident that God is with us and therefore life is good.

FAMILY TIES

Read Mark 3:31-35.

*"[Jesus] said, 'Here are my mother and my brothers!
Whoever does God's will is my brother and sister and
mother'" (vv. 34-35).*

Baylor legend Lawrence Elkins helped shape the future of college football after he had been shaped by his family.

Inducted into the Texas Sports Hall of Fame in 2010, Elkins was All-America in 1964. In an era when running attacks ruled the day, Baylor coach John Bridgers used a pro-style offense. Nobody had ever seen a passing combination like quarterback Don Trull and Elkins, who set a national record in 1963 with 70 catches for 783 yards. His 70 catches stood as the record until 2002. "Our passing attack was so far ahead of everybody," Trull once said.

As the youngest of ten children, Elkins knew about hard work, perseverance, and living large. It was all a part of his upbringing. His father was gassed in World War I, receiving a pension of $61 to go with his odd jobs. "Without that pension, we would have starved to death," Lawrence once said.

His mother had formerly been married to a man legendary as the Santa Claus bank robber. He had robbed a bank in 1927 while wearing a Santa Claus suit. His gang was caught when their car ran out of gas, and he was hanged.

For young Lawrence, football meant getting tough or dying. He learned from two older brothers, who would "throw the ball at me as hard as they could. I got a lot of bloody noses. I don't think I quit crying until I was 16."

With his speed, his toughness, and his savvy, Elkins developed into a star receiver recruited by most of the Southwest's football powers, including Texas. He chose the Bears because of their pro-style offense.

Shaped by his family, Lawrence Elkins shaped college football, providing a glimpse of the game's future.

Some wit said families are like fudge, mostly sweet with a few nuts. You can probably call the names of your sweetest relatives, whom you cherish, and of the nutty ones too, whom you mostly try to avoid at a family reunion.

Like it or not, you have a family, and that's God's doing. God cherishes the family so much that he chose to live in one as a son, a brother, and a cousin.

One of Jesus' more startling actions was to redefine the family. No longer is it a single household of blood relatives or even a clan or a tribe. Jesus' family is the result not of an accident of birth but rather a conscious choice. All those who do God's will are members of Jesus' family.

What a startling and downright wonderful thought! You have family members out there you don't even know who stand ready to love you just because you're part of God's family.

[Elkins] drove up to campus with his ma and pa in a '48 Chevy. [He] was wearing a straw hat. They were like the Real McCoys.
 — *Running back Clint Mitchell on Lawrence Elkins' family*

**For followers of Jesus, family comes not
from a shared ancestry but from a shared faith.**

TRADITIONS

Read Mark 7:1-13.

"You have let go of the commands of God and are holding on to the traditions of men" (v. 8).

Phil Bennett wanted some more "football playin' fools" so a Baylor tradition could be established.

As the Baylor defensive coordinator worked with his charges during the spring of 2014, he looked both to the future and back to the 2013 season. That's because he wanted his players to repeat or exceed what his "football playin' fools" did in the unforgettable championship season.

Understandably, much of the attention Baylor football received for its accomplishments in 2013 focused on the explosive offense that led the nation. But Bennett's defense was charged with getting the ball back to quarterback Bryce Petty and his cohorts as quickly as it could in the best possible location. The basic philosophy was a simple one: "Stops and turnovers and punts lead to points." "It's takeaways, it's red zone, it's three-and-outs and it's scoring. Get them the ball," Bennett explained.

How well did the defense do? It "was about as good as it gets on those fronts" in 2013. The defense was in the top 10 by forcing 29 turnovers, second-most in the Big 12. No team in the nation forced more three-and-out possessions (63) than did the Bears.

That's why Bennett spent his spring looking ahead and looking back. On their way to the practice field each day during the

BEARS

spring, the defensive players smacked the white "Be the Standard" sign hanging on the chain-link fence. The standard is that established in 2013, and the bar is set high.

Establishing a tradition is the defense's goal, no matter which of what he calls his "football playin' fools" Bennett plugs in.

You encounter traditions practically everywhere in your life. Your workplace may have casual Friday. Your family may have a particular way of decorating the Christmas tree, or it may gather to celebrate Easter at a certain family member's home.

Your church probably has traditions also. A particular type of music, for instance. Or how often you celebrate Communion. Or the order of worship.

Jesus knew all about religious tradition; after all, he grew up in the Church. He understood, though, the danger that lay in allowing tradition to become a religion in and of itself, and in his encounter with the Pharisees, Jesus rebuked them for just that.

Jesus changed everything that the world had ever known about faith. This included the traditions that had gradually arisen to define the way the Jews of his day worshipped. Jesus declared that those who truly worship God do not do so by simply observing various traditions, but rather by establishing a meaningful, deep-seated personal relationship with him.

Tradition in our faith life is useful only when it helps to draw us closer to God.

I don't want to say tradition, but we've started building expectancy.
— Phil Bennett on the high standards for his defense

**Religious tradition has value only when it serves
to strengthen our relationship with God.**

THE GOOD OLD DAYS

Read Psalm 102.

*"My days vanish like smoke; . . . but you remain the same,
and your years will never end" (vv. 3, 27).*

The "good old days" weren't really that good for women's basketball at Baylor.

The Baylor women started playing what was then called "extramural" athletics in the fall of 1961. Jeanne Nowlin, who would eventually serve as Baylor's assistant athletic director for women's sports, recalled "simply getting into a friend's car or van to go and play against other schools." The "modern" era of Baylor women's basketball can be said to have begun in 1973 with the awarding of the first scholarship to a woman, basketball legend Suzie Snider.

They were the Bearettes back then, and scholarships and frills were rare. Sue Turner headed to college in the fall of 1972 after lettering three years in high school. She simply called coach Olga Fallen – who would eventually "be seen clearly as the mother of Baylor's" women's intercollegiate program – and said she wanted to play basketball. "She told me when to show up for practice so I did, and was part of the team," Turner recalled. "As far as I know, she didn't hold tryouts."

According to Turner, the Bearettes were supplied with uniforms and money for lodging at overnight tournaments. "Other than that," she said, "the girls were on their own. They drove their own cars all over Texas to take on other teams, paying for their own gas and food along the way." Turner recalled that the women weren't awarded letters though they played for Baylor.

Pam Bowers, who took over as the second head basketball coach in 1979, washed the girls' jerseys and drove the team bus during her tenure. Even into the 1990s, head coach Sonja Hogg didn't have a VCR to watch game tapes and the band didn't play at the women's games. Season tickets weren't sold, a tip-off club didn't exist, and the media virtually ignored the program.

The "good old days" have obviously gotten a lot better for women's basketball at Baylor.

It's a brutal truth that time just never stands still. The current of your life sweeps you along until you realize one day you've lived long enough to have a past. Part of it you cling to fondly. The stunts you pulled with your high-school buddies. Your first apartment. That dance with your first love. That special vacation. Those "good old days."

You hold on relentlessly to the memory of those old, familiar ways because of the stability they provide in our uncertain world. They will always be there even as times change and you age.

Another constant exists in your life too. God has been a part of every event in your life that created a memory because he was there. He's always there with you; the question is whether you ignore him or make him a part of your day.

A "good old day" is any day shared with God.

I just walked in there and played because I wanted to.
— Sue Turner on the 'good old days' of Baylor women's basketball

Today is one of the "good old days"
if you share it with God.

GOAL ORIENTED

Read 1 Peter 1:3-12.

"For you are receiving the goal of your faith, the salvation of your souls" (v. 9).

Once upon a time, the Baylor Bears and their fans were ecstatic because the football team had become eligible for a bowl game. Funny how things change.

On Oct. 23, 2010, Baylor defeated Kansas State for the sixth win of the season. That meant the team had accomplished the goal it had set before the season began: win at least the six games required to be eligible for a bowl game. (See Devotion No. 23.)

The win touched off a wild celebration. Fans "stampeded out of the stands [and] partied on the field with the Baylor players." Special edition newspapers appeared, trumpeting in bold head-lines "Bowl Bound."

Once that goal was accomplished, though, Art Briles and his players set their collective minds on bigger accomplishments. A bowl game became not a goal but an expectation. The sights were now set on a Big 12 championship with its automatic slot in a BCS bowl game and on the national championship.

Thus, hardly any celebration at all followed Baylor's 71-7 dis-mantling of Iowa State on Oct. 19, 2013. Barely any notice was taken of the fact that the win was the Bears' sixth of the season and they were eligible for their fourth straight bowl game.

The win wasn't taken for granted, but the bowl appearance

certainly was. "It's big time to go to a bowl," quarterback Bryce Petty conceded. "It's a huge accomplishment because our goal before the season was six [wins] after six [games]. But it doesn't stop here."

That attitude explained why the reaction after the blowout victory that upped the team's record to 6-0 was just business as usual. No longer would an appearance in just any bowl mean the season was successful. The Bears had come a long way in three seasons and so had their goals.

What are your goals for your life? Have you ever thought them out as the Bears do before each season? Or do you just shuffle along living for your paycheck and whatever fun you can seek out instead of pursuing some greater purpose?

Now try this one: What is the goal of your faith life? You go to church to worship God. You read the Bible and study God's word to learn about God and how God wants you to live. But what is it you hope to achieve? What is all that stuff about? For what purpose do you believe that Jesus Christ is God's son?

The answer is actually quite simple. The goal of your faith life is your salvation, and this is the only goal in life that matters. Nothing you will ever seek is as important or as eternal as getting into Heaven and making sure that everybody you know and love will be there too one day.

If I ever accomplish [a goal], I'll set a higher goal and go after that.
— *Bobby Bowden*

**The most important goal of your life
is to get to Heaven and to help as many people
as you can to get there one day too.**

HEART OF THE MATTER

Read Matthew 6:19-24.

"Store up for yourselves treasures in heaven . . . . For where your treasure is, there your heart will be also" (vv. 20, 21).

Grant Teaff went with his heart instead of his head. Baylor fans have been forever grateful.

In 1971, only three seasons after replacing John Bridgers as head football coach, Baylor was once again looking for a gridiron boss. A disparity between the financial resources of the Waco private school and those of the state institutions of the Southwest Conference meant that the job was not one coaches exactly sought out. The word in the locker rooms was that more than a dozen assistant and head coaches turned the job down. Baylor Athletic Director Jack Patterson eventually turned to the University of New Mexico and hired its head coach, Rudy Feldman.

One coach who had no interest in Baylor was Grant Teaff. He was the head coach at Angelo State University, and "My plan was to become the head coach at Texas Tech" eventually. Thus, when his wife, Donell, and he saw on television that Feldman had been hired, Teaff said he was glad Patterson had found his man. Donell's reply was, "You are going to Baylor." Teaff laughed and said, "Baylor has a coach." Donell just repeated what she had said.

The next day, Feldman changed his mind and resigned. Patterson knew where to turn. Teaff and he were friends from Teaff's track coaching days at McMurry College. He made the call. "I had absolutely no interest in the job," Teaff said, but the AD convinced him to at least come for a visit. That evening, Donell and he flew to Waco.

"Coach Patterson's sincerity and his deep concern for the university touched me in a unique way," Teaff later said. "My head was saying 'no,' but I found my heart saying 'yes.'"

To ignore his head and go with his heart, Teaff had to take a leap of faith. "I stepped out on faith alone and accepted the job," was the way he put it. Twenty-one seasons later, he retired as the winningest coach in Baylor football history.

As Grant Teaff did, we often face decisions in life that force us to choose between our heart and our head. Our head says take that job with the salary increase; our heart says don't relocate because the kids are doing so well. Our head declares now is not the time to start a relationship; our heart insists that we're in love.

We wrestle with our head and our heart as we determine what matters the most to us. When it comes to the ultimate priority in our lives, though, our head and our heart tell us it's Jesus.

What that means for our lives is a resolution of the conflict we face daily: that of choosing between the values of our culture and a life of trust in and obedience to God. The two may occasionally be compatible, but when they're not, our head tells us what Jesus wants us to do; our heart tells us how right it is that we do it.

[Grant] Teaff came to Baylor with the fervor of a revival preacher.
— Writer Alan J. Lefever

**In our struggle with competing value systems,
our head and our heart lead us to follow Jesus.**

TURNAROUND

Read Acts 9:1-22.

"All those who heard him were astonished and asked, 'Isn't he the man who raised havoc in Jerusalem among those who call on this name?'" (v. 21)

The Baylor softball team was within one hit of being mercy-ruled out of the Women's College World Series. That was before the Bears pulled off the greatest turnaround in series history.

On May 31, 2014, Baylor met Kentucky in an elimination game. With two outs in the top of the sixth inning, the Bears trailed 7-0, and the eighth run — which would have invoked college softball's mercy rule to end the game unless Baylor could score in its half of the sixth — stood on second base.

The run didn't score but no matter. No team in the history of the softball world series had ever come from seven runs down to win a game. After the game, Bear coach Glenn Moore conceded that at the time "the only Moore in the dugout with complete confidence the team would win was his son." That Baylor scored three runs in the bottom of the sixth meant little except that the teams would play a seventh inning. It really didn't seem to matter either when Heather Stearns set the Wildcats down in order in the top of the seventh. But it all mattered.

In the bottom of the seventh, Ari Hawkins led off with a home run. 7-4. With one out, Sarah Smith doubled home Holly Holl. 7-5. Jordan Strickland walked, and then with two outs, Robin Landrith blasted an opposite-field double to tie the game. As every Bear fan in the place went nuts, it was on to extra innings.

After Kentucky failed to score, Kaitlyn Thumann, Baylor's leading hitter all season, lined a double to start the inning. Moore told Hawkins to bunt. She got it down, and when the throw to first bounded into right field, Thumann came around to score.

8-7. Baylor's historic turnaround was complete.

We often look for some means or some spark we can use to turn our lives around. Oh, we may not be headed to prison or bankrupt or plagued by an addiction. Maybe we can't find a purpose to our life and are just drifting.

Still, our situation often seems untenable to us. We sink into gloom and despair, wasting our time, our emotions, and our energy by fretting about how bad things are and how they will never get better. How in the world can we turn things around?

Turn to Jesus; as the old hymn urges, trust and obey him. If it's that simple, then why hesitate? Well, it's also that complicated as Paul discovered when he experienced one of the most dramatic turnarounds in history. To surrender to Jesus is to wind up with a new life and to wind up with a new life, we have to surrender to Jesus. We have to give up control.

What's to lose? After all, if we're looking for a way to turn our lives around, we're not doing such a good job of running things. What's to gain? Life worth living, both temporal and eternal.

I won't forget that one until I forget who I am.
— Baylor coach Glenn Moore on the turnaround vs. Kentucky

**A life in need of turning around
needs Jesus at the wheel.**

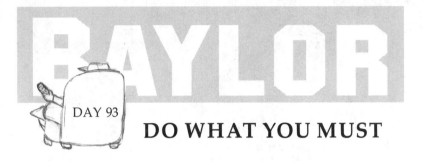

DAY 93

DO WHAT YOU MUST

Read 2 Samuel 12:1-15a.

"The Lord sent Nathan to David" (v. 1).

In the end, Baylor quarterback Bryce Petty did what he had to: He turned the game over to another player to complete one of the greatest comebacks in Baylor history.

On Oct. 11, 2014, the 5th-ranked Bears hosted the 9th-ranked Horned Frogs of TCU. The contest was an instant classic, but for quite a few Baylor fans it looked like anything but as the last half wore on. Some of them, in fact, gave up and made their way for the exits early in the fourth quarter.

They had good reason at the time. With 11:38 left in the game, TCU had a seemingly insurmountable 58-37 lead. Petty wasn't bothered at all. "I told our guys we weren't going to lose that game," he later said.

It took only 59 seconds for the Bears to make it 58-44 with running back Devin Chafin scoring from the 7. The next Baylor possession covered 92 yards and took only 1:23 off the clock. It ended with Petty hitting Antwan Goodley with a touchdown pass from 28 yards out. 58-51. After another defensive stop, the Baylor lightning struck again. 91 yards in 59 seconds, Petty to Corey Coleman for a 25-yard touchdown. The game was tied.

The Bears had scored too quickly, though, leaving 4:42 on the clock. Sure enough, the Frogs moved to the Baylor 45 where they faced a fourth-and-3 with 1:17 left. They chose to go for it, but a

BEARS

pass was incomplete; the ball belonged to Baylor.

Now the Frogs had given Petty and the Bears too much time. With 4 seconds left, he trotted off the field having done all he could and leaving the outcome in the hands of kicker Chris Callahan. He had thrown for a career-best 510 yards and six TDs.

Petty gave Callahan some encouragement and then did the only thing he could: He paced the sideline, too nervous to watch. Callahan, too, did what he had to. His 28-yard field goal was good, and Baylor had an incredible 61-58 comeback win.

You've had to do some things in your life that you had to, like Bryce Petty, who probably preferred not to be on the sideline when the winning points were scored against TCU. Maybe when you put your daughter on severe restriction, broke the news of a death in the family, or underwent surgery. You plowed ahead because you knew it was for the best or you had no choice.

Nathan surely didn't want to confront King David and tell him what a miserable reprobate he'd been, but the prophet had no choice: Obedience to God overrode all other factors. Of all that God asks of us in the living of a godly life, obedience is perhaps the most difficult. After all, our history of disobedience stretches all the way back to the Garden of Eden. The problem is that God expects obedience not only when his wishes match our own but also when they don't.

Obedience to God is a way of life, not a matter of convenience.

I don't think I could play kicker. That's too much pressure
— Bryce Petty on turning the TCU game over to Chris Callahan

Obedience requires being ready to do
whatever God asks, whatever you must do for him.

TAKE A CHANCE

Read Matthew 4:18-22.

"[A]nd immediately they left the boat and their father and followed him" (v. 22).

Don Trull took a chance on a school he'd never heard of and a promise from its head coach. It worked out right well for him.

Hordes of recruiters weren't exactly knocking down his front door despite Trull's emergence as a star quarterback his senior season of high school in 1959. But Baylor had a new head coach in John Bridgers, who had worked the past two seasons with the Baltimore Colts and a quarterback named Johnny Unitas. He intended to bring that offense to Waco, and he was interested in young Trull.

So when Bridgers invited the kid from Oklahoma City to come down for a visit, he decided to go even though he had never even heard of Baylor. Trull liked the campus, and when Bridgers told him he was installing the Colts' offense, Trull was sold. "I idolized Johnny Unitas, so I figured that was the best thing for me," he said.

For a while, though, it looked as if Trull had made a mistake when he took a chance on this Texas school. He was fourth or fifth string on the freshman team when he arrived. "I had been on the bottom of the barrel before," he said, "but not four bottoms down." He talked to his parents about leaving, but they told him to take a chance by staying and doing his best.

That best turned out to be pretty good. In the spring, he began to draw the coaches' attention, and in his last two seasons in Waco, Trull flourished in Bridgers' offense, rewriting the Baylor record books. He was All-America in 1963 and went on to a pro career. In 2013, he was inducted into the College Football Hall of Fame. The Texas Sports Hall of Fame came shortly afterwards.

Our lives are the sum total of the chances we have taken — or have not taken — along the way. Every decision we make every day involves taking a chance. Maybe it will work out for the better; maybe it won't. We won't know unless we take a chance.

On the other hand, our regrets often center on the chances we pass by. The missed chance that has the most destructive and devastating effect on our lives comes when we fail to follow Jesus. He calls us all to surrender to him, to commit to him exactly as he called Simon, Andrew, James, and John.

What they did is unsettling. Without hesitation, without telling Jesus to give them time to think about it or wrap up the loose ends of their lives or tell all their friends good-bye, they walked away from a productive living and from their families. They took a chance on this itinerant preacher.

So must we. What have we got to lose? Nothing worthwhile. What have we got to gain? Everlasting life with God.

If that's not worth taking a chance on, nothing is.

I had heard of Elgin Baylor and Baylor wristwatches, but I had never heard of Baylor.
— Don Trull on the chance he took in going to Waco

To take a chance and surrender our lives to Jesus is to trade hopelessness and death for hope and life.

THE END

Read Revelation 22:1-17.

"I am the Alpha and the Omega, the First and the Last, the Beginning and the End" (v. 13).

Robert Griffin III cried while his teammates celebrated joyously. When he saw that, head coach Art Briles knew: The legendary quarterback's time at Baylor had ended.

On Dec. 29, 2011, the Bears took on the Washington Huskies in the Alamo Bowl. Speculation was widespread that this would be the last college game for Baylor's Heisman-Trophy winning junior quarterback.

The game was a wild one. "That was crazy," was the way Briles described it. In the highest scoring regulation game in collegiate bowl history, the Bears clawed the Huskies 67-56. It was Baylor's first win in a bowl game since 1992.

By Griffin's superhero standards, he had something of an unremarkable night. For mere mortals, he was excellent, hitting on 24 of 33 passes for 295 yards and one touchdown while rushing for another score. Record-setting senior running back Terrance Ganaway (See Devotion No. 8.) was named the game's offensive MVP after, rushing for 200 yards and five touchdowns. His last score came on a 43-yard run with 2:28 left that locked up the win.

The game had barely ended when the Baylor fans, well aware of what was going on, began their chant: "One more year! One more year!" They shouted as Griffin paraded the game's trophy around the field before taking it to the front row of the stands where his mother sat. "I want Baylor nation to enjoy this," Griffin said. "It's not about me."

The players certainly enjoyed it. The Baylor locker room was joyous chaos after the game. "Players were chanting, dancing, hugging, and generally reveling in the excitement" of the long-awaited bowl win. Briles was right in the middle of it all.

So inevitably one player's reaction caught his attention. Amid all the euphoria, Griffin was alone and crying. Briles said he knew right then that RGIII had made his decision: He was gone.

Robert Griffin III's legendary career at Baylor is just another example of one of life's basic truths: Everything ends. Even the stars have a life cycle, though admittedly it's a rather lengthy one. Erosion eventually will wear a boulder to a pebble. Life itself is temporary; all living things have a beginning and an end.

Within the framework of our own lifetimes, we experience endings. Loved ones, friends, and pets die; relationships fracture; jobs dry up; our health, clothes, lawn mowers, TV sets – they all wear out. Even this world as we know it will end.

But one of the greatest ironies of God's gift of life is that not even death is immune from the great truth of creation that all things must end. That's because through Jesus' life, death, and resurrection, God himself acted to end any power death once had over life. In other words, because of Jesus, the end of life has ended. Eternity is ours for the claiming.

My advice to Baylor fans would be to let him go. It's time.
— Sportswriter Brice Cherry on RGIII after the Alamo Bowl

Everything ends; thanks to Jesus Christ, so does death.

THE END   191

NOTES
(by Devotion Day Number)

1   the first documented football game . . . but rather "rugby modified.": Alan J. Lefever, *The History of Baylor Sports* (Waco: Baylor University Press, 2013), p. 27.

1   In 1896, the Baylor student . . . intramural football games: Lefever, p. 27.

1   These garnered such widespread . . . it was soon dropped.: Lefever, p. 29.

2   That first swing from . . . Mike Tyson right cross.": John Werner, "#4 Baylor 63, Texas Tech 34," *Waco Tribune-Herald*, Nov. 17, 2013, www.wacotrib.com/sports/baylor/football/baylor-texas-tech-resilient-to-boot/article.

2   "the defense looked lost. The offense sputtered.": Brice Cherry, "No Hint of Panic in Trailing Bears," *Waco Tribune-Herald*, Nov. 17, 2013, www.wacotrib.com/sports/baylor/football/brice-cherry-no-hint-of-panic-in-trailing-bears/article.

2   "We knew this was going to be a dogfight,": Werner, "#4 Baylor 63."

2   It's impressive when you're . . . and finish like we did.: Werner, "#4 Baylor 63."

3   "We're getting embarrassed on . . . avalanche and a burial.: Grant Wahl, "Choice Words," *Sports Illustrated*, Dec. 12, 2005, sportsillustrated.cnn.com/vault/article/magazine/MAG1114641/index.htm.

3   Mulkey first said nothing; . . . rediscovered their groove.": Wahl, "Choice Words."

3   "We were getting ripped . . . the table for us.: Wahl, "Choice Words."

4   At the last minute, . . . a shoeshine kit.: "Program History," *2013 Baylor Football Media Almanac*, p. 89, www.baylorbears.com/sports/m-footbl/13-media-almanac.html.

5   he also had an occasional mean streak.: Nick Eatman, *Art Briles Looking Up* (Chicago: Triumph Books, 2013), p. 239.

5   He had grown up . . . he did playing football.: Eatman, p. 239.

5   Watkins' first conversation . . . he understood me, either."Eatman, p. 240.

5   Pleased with his progress, . . . they keep talking about?": Eatman, p. 240.

5   I didn't know if they . . . different than Canadians.: Eatman, p. 240.

6   "this half-pint with the tart tongue": "Program History," p. 87.

6   who "came into the . . . from the sidelines.": "Program History," p. 86.

6   A report circulated in . . . I'll get you a raise.": "Program History," p. 87.

6   when Bridges approached . . . luck and good day.": Lefever, p. 33.

6   That was the first . . . he didn't like me.: "Program History," p. 87.

7   In the seventh and eighth . . . "I was bad,".: John Werner, "NCAA Preview," *Year of the Bear* (Waco: Pediment Publishing, 2012), pp. 80-81.

7   he set a Big 12 record by making the first twenty shots he attempted.: Werner, "NCAA Preview," p. 81.

7   I loved it here as a freshman.: Werner, "NCAA Preview," p. 81.

8   "arguably the most prolific running back in school history.": "Terrance Ganaway," *baylorbears.com*, www.baylorbears.com/sports/m-footbl/mtt/ganaway_terrance00.html.

8   Entering the 2011 season, . . . any more football.: Eatman, p. 257.

8   After a talk with . . . worked hard at it.: Eatman, p. 257.

8   A newfound focus showed up on the field.: Eatman, p. 258.

8   Each day, the head coach . . . a big night" against Missouri.: Eatman, p. 258.

8   It's going to be a . . . You should.: Eatman, p. 258.

9   Not many schools were . . . at me was his intensity.": Jerry Hill, "Baylor Football Legend: Mike Singletary," *baylorbears.com*, Oct. 4, 2013, www.baylorbears.com/sports/m-footbl/spec-rel/100413aaa.html.

9   His trademark was "the . . . extra helmets on hand: Hill, "Baylor Football Legend."

9   I was just glad it wasn't my head.: Hill, "Baylor Football Legend."

10   "It was amazing, considering he only took three jumps,": "Obi Leaps for Bears' 1st National Title Since 2009," *Waco Tribune-Herald*, March 16, 2014, www.wacotrib.com/sports/baylor/baylor_track_and_field/obi-leaps-for-bears-st-national-title-since/article.

10   "I almost wanted to . . . the last jump was done.": "Obi Wins NCAA Indoor Triple Jump Crown," *baylorbears.com*, March 15, 2014, www.baylorbears.com/sports/c-track/recaps/031514aab.html.

10   the national champion passed . . . a whole bunch of hugs.: "Obi Leaps."

10   I was competing in . . . with a big jump.: "Obi Wins NCAA."

11   "once-in-a-generation . . . four years in Waco.": "Robert Griffin III," *baylorbears.com*, www.
      baylorbears.com/sports/m-footbl/mtt/griffiniiirobert00.html.

11   The coaches really started . . . Griffin decided against Baylor.: Pablo S. Torre, "Back of All
      Trades," *Sports Illustrated*, Sept, 26, 2011, sportsillustrated.cnn.com/vault/article/
      magazine/MAG1190636/index.htm.

11   He's coming. We finally got your hurdler.: Torre, "Back of All Trades."

12   head coach Grant Teaff spotted . . . for the second half.: Grant Teaff, "2 Seasons That
      Changed Baylor Football Forever," *Waco Tribune-Herald*, Sept. 22, 2013, www.waco
      trib.com/sports/baylor/football/grant-teaff-seasons-that-changed-baylor-football-
      forever/article.

12   "The championship was on the line,": Luke Blount, "Bears Upset No. 12 Longhorns 34-24,"
      baylorbears.com, Nov. 9, 2007, www.baylorbears.com/sports/m-footbl/spec-rel/110907
      aaa.html.

12   We have a great . . . back in a game.: Teaff, "2 Seasons."

13   Size is overrated in all sports.": Jason Orts, "Lady Bears Freshman Nina Davis Overlooked
      No More," *Waco Tribune-Herald*, Feb. 9, 2014, www.wacotrib.com/sports/baylor/lady_
      bears_basketball/lady-bears-freshman-nina-davis-overlooked-no-more/article.

13   "I'm sure there were . . . top of her head.": Orts, "Lady Bears Freshman."

13   "If you can play, . . . five-player class: Orts, "Lady Bears Freshman."

13   "with the soul of someone 6-4,": Orts, "Lady Bears Freshman."

13   I might be small, but I feel like I play big.: Orts, "Lady Bears Freshman."

14   "the greatest upset in . . . the Southwest Conference.": Dave Campbell, "Veteran Writer
      Remembers Baylor Great Jack Wilson," *baylorbears.com*, April 25, 2001, www.baylor
      bears.com/sports/m-footbl/spec-rel/042501aaa.html.

14   "He was absolutely the . . . Beautiful muscle development.": Campbell, "Veteran Writer
      Remembers."

14   *Life* magazine called them . . . SMU vs. A&M.: Campbell, "Veteran Writer Remembers."

14   "as the afternoon shadows lengthened and the crowd grew silent,": Campbell, "Veteran
      Writer Remembers."

14   In 1956, the tie . . . conference's first forty years.: Campbell, "Veteran Writer Remembers."

14   A wounded warrior . . . himself and his team.: Campbell, "Veteran Writer Remembers."

15   "This was the year the unbelievable became believable at Baylor.": John Werner, "After-
      word," *Year of the Bear* (Waco: Pediment Publishing, 2012), p. 139.

15   the Year of the Bear: Dave Campbell, "Foreword," *Year of the Bear* (Waco: Pediment Publish-
      ing, 2012), p. 7.

15   I thought this might . . . it would be like this.: Campbell, "Foreword," p. 5.

16   Four minutes into the . . . had beaten Oklahoma State.: John Werner, "Trophy Case," *Waco
      Tribune-Herald*, Dec. 8, 2013, www.wacotrib.com/sports/baylor/football/trophy-case-
      bears-brave-bitter-cold-for-big-title-bcs/article.

16   "No one had to say . . . and fight for it.": Werner, "Trophy Case."

16   Before the game ended, . . . presented the championship trophy.: Werner, "Trophy Case."

16   The fans who have . . . cried more than me.: Werner, "Trophy Case."

17   In 2007, when she . . . Baylor in the series.: John Werner, "Time to Shine," *Waco Tribune-
      Herald*, May 31, 2011, www.wacotrib.com/sports/baylor/softball/john-werner-time-to-
      shine-for-canion-lady-bears/article.

17   "To actually get a . . . feeling in the world,": Werner, "Time to Shine."

17   It's crazy how dreams come true.: Werner, "Time to Shine."

18   "You're dadgum right we wanted . . . no track around it.": John Werner, "Floyd Casey's 1st
      Tenants Share Tales of 1950 Triumphs," *Waco Tribune-Herald*, Aug. 31, 2013, www.
      wacotrib.com/sports/baylor/football/floyd-casey-s-st-tenants-share-tales-of-
      triumphs/article.

18   "the Baylor players had never . . . difference was night and day.": Werner, "Floyd
      Casey's 1st Tenants."

18   After the game, head . . . pomp and circumstance.: Werner, "Floyd Casey's
      1st Tenants."

18   It was magnificent. . . . is going to be awesome.: Werner, "Floyd Casey's 1st Tenants."

19   Smith was frustrated and . . . Briles was ready.: Eatman, p. 225.

19   He told Smith that if . . . a car or a Cadillac,": Eatman, p. 226.

19   We didn't worry about . . . take care of itself.: Eatman, p. 226.

20   "the best worst pass . . . in the wind forever.": John Werner, "Last Year's Baylor Comeback," *Waco Tribune-Herald*, Nov. 2, 2012, www.wacotrib.com/sports/baylor/john-werner-last-year-s-baylor-comeback-still/article.

20   "It was the biggest . . . right after the game.: Werner, "Last Year's Baylor Comeback."

20   I can't quite believe what I saw that afternoon.: Werner, "Last Year's Baylor Comeback."

21   Some of his buddies . . . he'd lost his mind.": John Werner, "DE McAllister Showing Doubters Wrong at Baylor," *Waco Tribune-Herald*, Oct. 5, 2013, www.wacotrib.com/sports/football/de-mcallister-showing-doubters-wrong-at-baylor/article.

21   "I trusted in Coach . . . than other schools.": Werner, "DE McAllister."

21   "I walked into his . . . 'Who is this guy?'": Werner, "DE McAllister."

21   never thought he'd go . . . the hang of it: Werner, "DE McAllister."

21   When I chose Baylor, my friends were making fun of me.: Werner, "DE McAllister."

22   "a quiet giant, both . . . about than tell you.": Janet Goreham, "Keeping Up with the Jones," *Sharing the Victory Magazine*, May 8, 2009, http://wwww.sharingthevictory.com/vslItemDisplay.1sp&objectID=AC8A85E2-99A5-4CD7.

22   She was cut from . . . a witness for God.": Goreham, "Keeping Up with the Jones."

22   She wore it while . . . "The Smiling Assassin.": Goreham, "Keeping Up with the Jones."

22   She'll smile at you and then just beat you bad.: Goreham, "Keeping Up with the Jones."

23   "the biggest win for the program in more than a decade.": Eatman, p. 249.

23   "Man, it really is that hard to be bowl eligible at Baylor,": Eatman, p. 249.

23   That was the day . . . over the proverbial hump.: Eatman, p. 249.

24   he was caught off . . . "Get in," Briles ordered.: Brandon Chatmon, "Future Is Now for Baylor's Hall, Cannon," *ESPN.com*, Sept. 12, 2014, http://espn.go.com/blog/big12/post/_/id/89158/future-is-now-for-baylors-hall-cannon.

24   I wasn't expecting to . . . was like, 'That's me!': Chatmon, "Future Is Now."

25   She played every game and . . . a nickname Mariah still carries.: Brice Cherry, "Lady Bears' 'Miracle' Mariah," *Waco Tribune-Herald*, Nov. 21, 2012, www.wacotrib.com/sports/baylor/brice-cherry-lady-bears-miracle-mariah-chandler-ever-grateful-for/article.

25   She prayed over me. . . . just bring her back.': Cherry, "Lady Bears' 'Miracle' Mariah."

26   "I just had this good . . . to go with him.": Eatman, p. 273.

26   Shortly before two-a-day . . . to the weight room.: Eatman, p. 273.

26   the coach told his . . . leader of the 2012 squad: Eatman, p. 274.

26   You're not going to be . . . and he lost his power.: Eatman, p. 274.

27   "the undisputed queen of women's basketball in Texas.": Barry Horn, "Baylor's Kim Mulkey Is Fierce," *Dallas Morning News*, March 9, 2012, www.dallasnews.com/sports/college-sports/baylor-bears/20120309-baylor-s-kim-mulkey-is-fierce-loving-and-loyal-but-dont-get-on-her-bad-side.ece.

27   "to make way for . . . for unanswered prayers,": Horn, "Baylor's Kim Mulkey Is Fierce."

27   The word for what . . . how low did I go?": Horn, "Baylor's Kim Mulkey Is Fierce."

28   During the 4-6 season of . . . on the college campus,": Morton Shamik, "A Coach Even the Faculty Likes," *Sports Illustrated*, Nov. 18, 1963, sports illustrated.cnn.com/vault/article/magazine/MAG1075384/index.htm.

28   John Dixon Bridgers is . . . be played for fun.: Shamik, "A Coach Even the Faculty Likes."

29   For many years, however . . . about the final score.": "Program History," *2013 Baylor Football Media Almanac*, p. 86, www.baylorbears.com/sports/m-footbl/13-media-almanac.html.

29   Only recently have both . . . an 11-10 win for TCU.: Lefever, p. 30.

30   "wiped out all those . . . wherever the two teams played.: John Werner, "Griffin Strike with 8 Seconds Left," *Year of the Bear*, p. 16.

30   "We were looking for . . . and we finally got it,": Werner, "Griffin Strike," pp. 16-17.

30   "I got hit and was . . . just won the game,": Werner, "Griffin Strike," p. 17.

30   For me personally, . . . this program changed.: John Werner, "Baylor's New Era," *Waco Tribune-Herald*, Nov. 7, 2013, www.wacotrib.com/sports/baylor/football/baylor-s-new-era-rg-s-last-minute-win-over/article.

BEARS

31   When a coach asked . . . this time to Milan.: Sam Borden, "The Basketball Player's Guide to the (European) Galaxy," *New York Times*, Jan. 12, 2014, www.nytimes.com/2014/01/13/sports/basketball/the-basketball-players-guide-to-the-european-galaxy.html?_r=2.

31   Darryl Middleton is by . . . in European basketball history.: Borden, "The Basketball Player's Guide."

32   "not some fly-by-night . . . of the highest order.": Will Parchman, "K-State's Heisman, BCS Title Hopes Cast Aside," *Waco Tribune-Herald*, Nov. 18, 2012. www.wacotrib.com/sports/baylor/will-parchman-k-state-s-heisman-bcs-title-hopes-cast/article.

32   "All week we believed . . . surprised when it happened.": Parchman, "K-State's Heisman, BCS Title Hopes Cast Aside."

32   We beat the socks off these guys.: John Werner, "Bears Turn College Foot-ball World on Its Ear," *Waco Tribune-Herald*, Nov. 18, 2012, www.wacotrib.com/sports/baylor/bears-turn-college-football-world-on-its-ear-with-blowout/article.

33   That brought Smith out . . . returned to the dugout.: Luke Blount, "Ryan LaMotta Waves Off Sun Devils," *baylorbears.com*, June 5, 2007, www.baylorbears.com/sports/m-basebl/spec-rel/060507aaa.html.

33   "(Waving off Smith) was a . . . it was my game.": Blount, "Ryan LaMotta Waves Off."

33   It didn't really come as . . . He wanted to win the game.: Blount, "Ryan LaMotta Waves Off."

34   "You're going to be . . . and 248 Baylor fans.": Grant Teaff, "Higher Stakes Yield Cheers at 'Big House,'" *Waco Tribune-Herald*, Oct. 5, 2013, www.wacotrib.com/sports/baylor/football/grant-teaff-remembers-higher-stakes-yield-cheers-at-big-house/article.

35   In 2000, her first year . . . waste of our time,": Kim Mulkey with Peter May, *Won't Back Down* (Philadelphia: Da Capo Press, 2007), p. 200.

35   while she was recuperating . . . and Danielle Crockrom.: Mulkey with May, pp. 200-201.

35   She also wanted to play for a coach who had been a point guard.: Dick Patrick, "Building Baylor Took Bit of Luck," *USA TODAY*, April 5, 2005, usatoday30.usatoday.com/sports/college/womensbasketball/tourney05/2005-04-04-baylor-recruits_x.htm.

35   The father of Jennifer . . . to make up her mind: Patrick, "Building Baylor."

35   In 2002, a woman strode . . . She was Abiola Wabara.: Patrick, "Building Baylor."

36   he had barely taken any snaps at practice.: Eatman, p. 241.

36   Briles called him over . . . trotted onto the field.: Eatman, p. 242.

36   he yanked Florence for . . . the same as Florence's.: Eatman, p. 243

37   "It was probably one of . . . ground to a halt.": John Werner, "Bears Anxious to Disprove Road Woes," *Waco Tribune-Herald*, Oct. 12, 2013, www.wacotrib.com/sports/baylor/football/bears-anxious-to-disprove-road-woes/article.

37   "It sets fire in your . . . we can win on the road.": Werner, "Bears Anxious."

37   "I like the fact we . . . a win on the road,": John Werner, "Grind-It-Out Win for Unbeaten Baylor, 35-25," *Waco Tribune-Herald*, www.wacotrib.com/sports/baylor/football/grind-it-out-win-for-unbeaten-baylor/article.

37   We came up here . . . get away with a win.: Werner, "Grind-It-Out Win."

38   in 1893, the Baylor . . . of a century ago.": Lefever, p. 17.

38   football "was brought to . . . and not by our request.": Lefever, p. 29.

39   Video replays, however, . . . packed up for the night.: Eatman, p. 280.

39   the players, coaches, and . . . score of the game: 49-19.: Eatman, p. 281.

39   [The replay officials] just . . . couldn't do anything.: Eatman, p. 280.

40   "shocked Baylor by coming . . . let me touch the ball,": John Werner, "Relieved Baylor Men," *Waco Tribune-Herald*, March 19, 2010, www.wacotrib.com/sports/baylor/mens_basketball/relieved-baylor-men-get-ncaa-gournament-gorilla-off-their-backs/article.

40   Obviously, the triangle-and-two affected us.: Werner, "Relieved Baylor Men."

41   He then enrolled at . . . the 2008 Summer Olympics.: Eatman, pp. 232-33.

41   "Had I qualified for . . . have ever played football.": Eatman, p. 233.

41   Not bad for an 18- . . . going to his senior prom.: Eatman, p. 233.

42   it was only in 1947 . . . serious about football.": "Program History," p. 88.

42   The excitable Broyles was . . . but which ones?": "Program History," p. 88.

43   "a week of misery" . . . call to Kyle Woods.: Grant Teaff, "1980 Team Turned Setback into a Comeback," *Waco Tribune-Herald*, Oct. 28, 2013,

195

www.wacotrib.com/sports/baylor/football/grant-teaff-remembers-team-turned-setback-into-a-comeback/article.

43   Woods reminded Teaff he . . . would ever stand again.: Teaff, "1980 Team."
43   Kyle [Woods] clearly demonstrated . . . an inspirational comeback.: Teaff, "1980 Team."
44   With deputy sheriff Bob . . . Player of the Year Award.: Lefever, p. 217.
44   The change was made . . . school was not over.: Lefever, p. 218.
44   "the symbolic gesture that . . . proved to be prophetic.": Lefever, p. 219.
44   with some members of the original team present: Laura A. Cadena, "Longest Softball Game to End," *The Lariat*, Sept. 14, 1995, www.baylor.edu/lariatarchives/news.php?action+story&story=8736.
44   We are thrilled to have Baylor softball back.: Cadena.
45   "quietly emerged as one of the Bears' biggest weapons,": Max Olson, "Baylor Finds Breakout Weapon in Norwood," *ESPN.com*, Nov. 19, 2013, espn.go.com/blog/ncfnation/post/_/id/88654/baylor-finds-breakout-weapon-in-norwood.
45   Levi was accustomed to . . . mountains or hills here,": Olson.
45   "bigger than football, . . . grow his faith was Baylor.: Olson.
45   It took a couple years for me to adjust.: Olson.
46   Steffanie Blackmon thought she . . . eaten much that day.: Calvin Watkins, "Ordeal Brings Blackmon Sisters Closer," *The Dallas Morning News*, April 3, 2005, nl.newsbank.com/nl-search/we/archives?p_action=doc&p_docid=10949C3B1352B659.
46   In May 2004, Steffanie . . . can be life-threatening.: Watkins.
46   She received no special . . . plenty of food and water.: Watkins.
46   "When Steffanie got sick, . . . want to lose her.": Watkins.
46   We thought we would lose her.: Watkins.
47   "downright hungry for a . . . against it and demurred.": "Program History,", p. 86.
47   "bitterness and confusion" . . . "Mr. Fouts' strip act.": "Program History, p. 86.
47   When you run trick . . . folks question your sanity.: Jim & Julie S. Bettinger, *The Book of Bowden* (Nashville: TowleHouse Publishing, 2001), p. 32.
48   "I never saw any doubt . . . there in the fourth quarter,": John Werner, "Baylor Overcomes No. 14 TCU in 50-48 Thriller," *Year of the Bear*, p. 9.
48   That last drive was . . . have zero momentum.: Werner, "Baylor Overcomes No. 14 TCU, p. 10.
49   "mostly preachers and people who couldn't get in the service.": Lefever, p. 71.
49   the undermanned squad . . . insurmountable challenge.": Randy Fiedler, "This Week in Baylor History: The Winless Basketball Season," *Baylor Arts & Sciences*, Feb. 18, 2013, blogs.baylor.edu/artsandsciences/2013/02/18.
49   "It must have been . . . season for the Bears,": Fiedler, "This Week in Baylor History."
49   "one of the greatest turnarounds in college basketball history.": Lefever, p. 72.
49   "a rousing crowd of . . . parade through downtown.: Fiedler, "This Week in Baylor History."
50   "a big, big game for us.": John Werner, "Bears Rein in Mustangs," *Waco Tribune-Herald*, Sept. 3, 2012, www.wacotrib.com/sports/football/baylor/bears-rein-in-mustangs-with-solid-defensive-effort/article.
50   "We were eager and . . . "We did that.": Werner, "Bears Rein in Mustangs."
50   We're going to keep this thing rolling at Baylor.: Werner, "Bears Rein in Mustangs."
51   a Gator guard said she . . . they're going to do.": Brice Cherry, "Baylor Lady Bears Are Swatting Everyone's Best Shot," *Waco Tribune-Herald*, March 20, 2012, www.wacotrib.com/sports/baylor/baylor-lady-bears-are-swatting-everyone-s-best-shot/article.
51   Kimetria Williams grabbed an . . . stepped back and watched.": Brice Cherry, "Griner Dunks as Lady Bears Slam Gator Jaws Shut, 76-57," *Waco Tribune-Herald*, March 21, 2012, www.wacotrib.com/sports/baylor/griner-drunks-as-lady-bears-slam-gator-jaws-shut/article.
51   During the on-court . . . "go win it all,": Cherry, ""Griner Dunks."
52   In August, Central Texas . . . the game was over.": Grant Teaff, "Memories Extend Beyond Field of Play," *Waco Tribune-Herald*, Nov. 7, 2013, www.wacotrib.com/sports/baylor/football/grant-teaff-memories-extend-beyond-field-of-play/article.
52   Well, yes, the pan . . . but not that hot.: Teaff, "Memories Extend."

53   during the week several . . . Baylor's two cub mascots.: Dave Campbell, "The Legendary Texas Sportswriter Recalls Some of Baylor's Best Games of the 1950s," *baylorbears.com*, Dec 9, 2013, www.baylorbears.com/sports/m-footbl/spec-rel/120913aab.html.

53   "really came of age" . . . special talent he was.": Campbell, "The Legendary Texas Sportswriter."

53   By then, the purloined . . . their car's back seat.: Campbell, "The Legendary Texas Sportswriter."

53   The bears enjoy what . . . respect and love them.: "Mascot History," *Baylor Bear Program*, www.baylor.edu/bear/index.php?id-18243.

54   the fan base knew . . . job was: Mike Singletary.: Eatman, p. 219.

54   Baylor AD Ian McCaw wasn't . . . top was Art Briles,": Eatman, p. 220.

54   The two met on . . . he had found his man.: Eatman, p. 220.

54   He knew Briles was . . . the Baylor football program.: Eatman, p. 220.

55   Rain was falling as . . . hampering the bus driver's vision: "The Immortal Ten," *baylorbears. com: Traditions*, baylorbears.com/trads/bay-immortal-10.html.

55   a railroad crossing obscured . . . the rear of the bus,: Lefever, p. 93.

55   killing ten of the 21 . . . saving his life.: "The Immortal Ten."

55   In a column the . . . as the Immortal Ten.: Lefever, p. 93.

55   The monument [honoring . . . have come to symbolize.: Lefever, p. 93.

56   Pass-happy offense run by . . . in a pass-happy league.": Andy Staples, "Fueled by Balanced Offense, Baylor Eyeing a Big 12 Title," *Sports Illustrated*, April 16, 2013, http://sports illustrated.cnn.com/college-football/news/20130416/baylor-offense.

56   "It's kind of a misconception we appreciate,": Staples.

56   People think of us as . . . we're going to get dirty.: Staples.

57   On the way down from . . . made the 1948 U.S. Olympic team.: John Henry, "Jack Robinson Returns to London," *Star-Telegram*, July 25, 2012, www.star-telegram.com/2012/07/ 25/4126689/jack-robinson-returns-to-london.html.

57   He kept the game ball.: Carson Cunningham, "'Jackie' Robinson Back at London Games," *Real Clear History*, July 23, 2012, www.realclearhistory.com/articles/2012/07/23/jackie_ robinson_back_at_london_games_30.html.

57   He was "awfully nervous" . . . from Texas, not California.: Henry, "Jack Robinson Returns to London."

57   Whoa, Sir, I'm from Texas.: Henry, "Jack Robinson Returns to London."

58   "the most exclusive club in college sports": John Werner, "Robert Griffin III Wins Baylor's First Heisman Trophy," *Year of the Bear*, p. 25.

58   This award is the . . . team and football program,": Werner, "Robert Griffin III Wins Baylor's First Heisman Trophy," p. 25.

58   Dressed in a black . . . with a red cape.: Werner, "Robert Griffin III Wins Baylor's First Heisman Trophy," p. 25.

58   the Superman pair turned . . . Letterman's late show.: Regina Dennis, "Heisman Winner's Superman Socks Soar in Popularity," *Year of the Bear*, p. 28.

58   During a separate interview . . . a pair of Elmo socks.: Dennis, p. 28.

58   he had enough pairs . . . SpongeBob Square Pants.: Lance Madden, "Robert Griffin III, Adidas Have a Lot of Sock Swag," *Forbes*, Sept. 21, 2012, www.forbes.com/sites/lance-madden/2012/09/21/robert-griffin-iii-adidas-have-a-lot-of-sock-swag/.

58   When you go to . . . suit, shoes and socks.: Werner, "Robert Griffin III Wins Baylor's First Heisman Trophy," p. 25.

59   That's like getting punched in the gut.: "Baylor Survives Late Blunder," *Dallas Morning News*, Feb. 17, 2014, www.dallasnews.com/sports/college-sports/baylor-bears/ 20140217/baylor-survives-late-blunder-tops-oklahoma-state-in-ot-cowboys-lose-seventh-straight.ece.

60   When Petty signed after the . . . he could lead the Bears: John Werner, "Understudy No More," *Waco Tribune-Herald*, Nov. 7, 2013, www.wacotrib.com/sports/baylor/football/ understudy-no-more-baylor-qb-petty-enjoys-spotlight/article.

60   "I'm not a very patient . . . on and off the field,": Werner, "Understudy No More."

60   God has had his . . . like it is now.: Werner, "Understudy No More."

61   Some local folks had him . . . coach never came.: "Program History," p. 87.

61	A group from Hillsboro . . . stood up in Hillsboro.": "Program History, p. 87.
62	"We got in at halftime . . . what was going on.": "Baylor Pummels Texas Tech," *ESPN*, Nov. 26, 2011, scores.espn.go.com/ncf/recap?gameId=313300239.
62	"Whatever I can do . . . "We need you, Nick,": Eatman, p. 261.
62	The team needed me . . . never regretted that decision: Eatman, p. 272.
63	Robertson joked at one point . . . room and say to them,": Graham Hays, "Makenzie, Kim Make Perfect Team," *ESPN*, Feb. 13, 2014, espn.go.com/womens-college-basketball/story/_/id10437949.
63	Robertson never seriously . . . coach only -- her mother.: Hays, "Makenzie, Kim Make Perfect Team."
63	"Anything she says to . . . before her senior season.: Hays, "Makenzie, Kim Make Perfect Team."
63	My mom's a very . . . I did something good.: Hays, "Makenzie, Kim Make Perfect Team."
64	the week of the Texas . . . I made the tackle!": Grant Teaff, "Final Games End, But Memories Last," *Waco Tribune-Herald*, Dec. 7, 2013, www.wacotrib.com/sports/baylor/football/grant-teaff-remembers-final-games-end-but-memories-last.
64	This is not up . . . in for one play.: Teaff, "Final Games End."
65	"which sent many of . . . all too familiar with.": Eatman, p. 229.
65	Ahmad Dixon, who wasn't . . .perception of Baylor.": Eatman, pp. 230-31.
65	The run was an . . . in need of a lift.: Eatman, p. 230.
66	"The Bears have been able . . . a beat on offense.": Mark Schlabach, "Briles' Offense Built Around Each QB," *ESPN*, Oct. 16, 2013, espn.go.com/college-football/story/_/id/9833069/baylor-coach-art-briles-builds-offense-quarterback.
66	Briles abandoned the playbook . . . load on the quarterbacks,": Schlabach, "Briles' Offense."
66	The less a quarterback has to think, the faster he can play.; Schlabach, "Briles' Offense."
67	"Baylor baseball under Sullivan . . . were a lot looser,": Kevin Sherrington, "Late Mickey Sullivan Kept Baylor Baseball on Top," *Dallas Morning News*, March 31, 2012, www.dallasnew.com/sports/columnists/kevin-sherrington/20120331-sherrington-late-mickey-sullivan-kept-baylor-baseball-on-top-with-casual-style.ece.
67	Sullivan wasn't much . . . "The dugout erupted,": Sherrington.
67	I wasn't soft on my boys. I was just for them.: Sherrington.
68	Teaff moved Mickey Elam . . . didn't call for volunteers.": Grant Teaff, "Wriggly Stunt Helps 1978 Baylor Team Turn Corner," *Waco Tribune-Herald*, Oct. 12, 2013, www.wacotrib.com/sports/baylor/football/grant-teaff-wriggly-stunt-helps-baylor-team-turn-corner/article.
68	Personally, I don't think . . . with our victory.: Teaff, "Wriggly Stunt."
69	"makes it a habit . . . player on his roster.": David Ubben, "Baylor Continuing to 'Shock' the World," *FoxSports.com*, Nov. 12, 2013, msn.foxsports.com/southwest/story/baylor-continuing-to-shock-the-world-111213.
69	this one caught on . . . nickname "StorkTheDork.": Ubben.
69	"I don't really know why," . . . reference or something.": Ubben.
69	Rashodrick Antoine Linwood . . . shortened it to "Shock.": Ubben.
69	I don't really know where that came from.: Ubben.
70	the player the basketball . . . Baylor handle him?: John Werner, "Baylor Men Knock Off No. 3," *Waco Tribune-Herald*, March 24, 2014, www.wacotrib.com/sports/baylor/mens-basketball/baylor-men-knock-off-no-creighton-to-advance/article.
70	The more pertinent . . . men had become.: Werner, "Baylor Men Knock Off No. 3."
70	"We got down defensively, and everybody did their assignment,": Werner, "Baylor Men Knock Off No. 3."
70	The coaches prepared us . . . good job of it.: Werner, "Baylor Men Knock Off No. 3."
71	The coaches said that . . . all passed on him.: John Werner, "New Baylor Linebacker," *Waco Tribune-Herald*, Sept. 14, 2012, www.wacotrib.com/sports/baylor/new-baylor-linebacker-showing-he-only-needed-chance/article.
71	"Northwood was the only place that would pay for my schooling,": Werner, "New Baylor Linebacker."
71	Phil Bennett instructed . . . before he left campus.: Werner, "New Baylor Linebacker."

198

71   The recruiting game is all . . . give him a chance.: Werner, "New Baylor Linebacker."

72   some Baylor students drove . . . snapped to attention.: Lefever, p. 33.

72   one Aggie was taken to . . . Texas Rangers intervened.: Lefever, p. 36.

72   A few weeks later, . . . suspended for four years.: Lefever, p. 36.

73   Melissa Jones "will go down . . . student-athletes in Baylor history.": "Melisa Jones, BA
      '11," *Baylor Magazine*, Summer 2011, www.baylor.edu/alumni/magazine/0904/news.
      php?action=story&stroy=95855.

73   During the next few minutes . . . the rest of the game.": David Pond, "Seeing the Light,"
      Sharing the Victory Magazine, March/April 2012, http://archives.fca.org/vsItemDisplay.1-
      sp?method=display.1sp?method=display&objectid=C0FF2C68-C29A-EE.

73   "It was a special moment for me to see God's work,": Pond, "Seeing the Light."

73   In 2012, she said of her . . . to adapt to it.": Irv Moss, "Colorado Classics," *The Denver Post*,
      Dec. 26, 2012, www.denverpost.com/ci_22259767/legacy-high-alum-melissa-jones-
      was-an-inspirational.

73   MJ didn't view . . . as a speed bump.: Pond, "Seeing the Light."

74   "was way more attractive . . . than people realized.": Eatman, p. 245.

74   The progress, however . . . Baylor head coach personally,: Eatman, p. 245.

74   Members of the Tech . . . he could in Waco.: Eatman, p. 245.

74   [Art Briles] was fully invested in Baylor.: Eatman, p. 246.

75   Stefan grew up in a . . . with a Baylor logo.": Raymond A. Partsch III,
      "Huber Has His Family Proud," *Beaumont Enterprise*, Dec. 24, 2013, www.beaumont
      enterprise.com/news/article/huber-has-his-family-proud-to-sport-colors-of-5090840.

75   "If I didn't get . . . ready for the light,": Partsch.

75   proudly wore Baylor green "because that is where my son goes.": Partsch.

75   Dad talked with me a lot and wanted me to push myself to be better.: John Werner, "Bay-
      lor's Huber Following Father's Lead," *Waco Tribune-Herald*, Sept 21, 2013, www.wa-
      cotrib.com/sports/baylor/football/baylors-huber-following-father-s-lead-in-football-
      medicine/article.

76   He was comfortable around his . . . pick up some pointers.: John Werner, "Baylor Receiver
      Lets Game Do His Talking," *Waco Tribune-Herald*, Oct. 15, 2010, www.wacotrib.com/
      sports/baylor/baylor-receiver-lets-game-do-his-talking/article.

76   I'm in an advanced interviewing class now,and I think it's helped.: Werner, "Baylor
      Receiver Lets Game Do His Talking."

77   The list and the quotes are from Jake Trotter's article, 'How the Baylor Bears Were Built,"
      which is found at *ESPN.com*, Feb. 16, 2015, http://espn.go.com/blog/big 12/post/_/
      id/96172/how-the-baylor-bears-were-built.

78   Cal missed three shots right before the buzzer: Jason Orts, "Baylor 75, Cal 56," *Waco
      Tribune-Herald*, March 24, 2014, www.wacotrib.com/sports/baylor/lady_bears_basket-
      ball/baylor-cal/lady-bears/come-alive/in-nd-half-to/article.

78   Sims hit a pair . . . floor for a layup: Orts, "Baylor 75, Cal 56."

78   "there was nothing the . . . from NBA range.: Orts, "Baylor 75, Cal 56."

78   I scored when I . . . the ball when I needed to.: Orts, "Baylor 75, Cal 56."

79   With the upset, the Bears jumped to No. 10 in the AP poll.: Lefever, p. 43.

79   Led by Jerry Haney, . . . finest hour,": "Bears Shutout Defending National Champion at
      Arkansas," baylorbears.com, Oct. 6, 2006, www.baylorbears.com/sports/m-footbl/
      spec-rel/100606aaa.html.

79   Arkansas head coach Frank . . . hard time beating Baylor.": "Bears Shutout Defending
      National Champion."

79   Inconsistency led Baylor to finish 5-5 for the season.: Luke Blount, "Baylor Upsets No. 7
      Syracuse," *baylorbears.com*, Sept. 7,2007, www.baylorbears.com/sports/m-footbl/spec-
      rel/090707aaa.html.

80   Beat-up, rain-soaked, and worn out.: Max Olson, "Baylor Shouldn't Apologize for 'Ugly'
      Win," *ESPN.com*, Nov. 224, 2014, http:espn.go.com/blog/big12/post/_/id/93073/baylor-
      shouldnt-apologize-for-ugly-win.

80   "a dreary and rainy night . . . of the Brazos River,": "Baylor Buries Oklahoma State,"
      ESPN.com, Nov. 23, 2014, http://scores.espn.go.com/ncf/recap?game
      Id=400547896.

80   By Baylor' standards, the drive was clearly "ugly.": Olson, "Baylor Shouldn't Apologize."

80   "As running backs, we . . . muddy, grimy games,": Olson, "Baylor Shouldn't Apologize."

80   When the drive ended, . . . his reaction was, "Wow!": Olson, "Baylor Shouldn't Apologize."

80   That was, uh . . . um, tiring.: Olson, "Baylor Shouldn't Apologize."

81   "shellshocked but not felled.": Will Parchman, "Ludy Saves Bears from Epic Collapse," *Waco Tribune-Herald*, March 20, 2011, www.wacotrib.com/sports/baylor/ludy-saves-bears-from-epic-collapse/article.

81   It's a good thing . . . there at the end.: Parchman, "Ludy Saves Bears."

82   The Monday morning morning before . . . gently into the end zone.: Grant Teaff, "Confident Bears Showed the Difference in '72," *Waco Tribune-Herald*, Sept. 7, 2013, www.wacotrib.com/sports/baylor/football/grant-teaff-confident-bears-showed-the-difference-in/article.

82   I heard from many . . . a 'Difference at Baylor.': Teaff, "Confident Bears Showed the Difference in '72."

83   Before the 1910 game, . . . flamboyant request and left.: "Program History," p. 86.

83   The raging and defiant [E.T.] Adams initially refused to go.: "Program History," p. 86.

84   Thus began a two-year . . . finally to Fort Worth.: Jeff Brown, "Spotlight: Cyril Richardson," *baylorbears.com*, Oct. 5, 2013, baylorbears.com/sports/m-footbl/mtt/richardson_cyril00.html.

84   He was behind . . . and he accepted.: Brown, "Spotlight."

84   My brother saw something in me that I didn't realize.: Brown, "Spotlight."

85   When he was 12, Austin . . . the court as possible.: Stephen Hawkins, "Blind Eye No Excuse for Baylor's Isaiah Austin," *boston.com*, Feb. 13, 2014, www.boston.com/sports/colleges/mens-basketball/2014/02/13-blind-eye-no-excuse-for-baylor-isaiah-austin.

85   He didn't tell Bear . . . then I can do it,': Hawkins, "Blind Eye No Excuse."

85   You can make it . . . make it your story.: Hawkins, "Blind Eye No Excuse."

86   Campbell began playing baseball . . . its Christian environment.: Brice Cherry, "Baylor Infielder Shrugs Off Junior Slump," *Waco Tribune-Herald*, May 21, 2010, www.wacotrib.com/sports/baylor/baylor-infielder-shrugs-off-junior-slump/article.

86   switched to a wooden . . . Cod Summer League.: Cherry, "Baylor Infielder."

86   "It was very frustrating,": Cherry, "Baylor Infielder."

86   "It taught me so . . . righteous rebirth" in 2010.: Cherry, "Baylor Infielder."

86   I found Christ on a . . . that year for anything.: Cherry, "Baylor Infielder."

87   "Our passing attack was so far ahead of everybody,": John Werner, "Baylor Legend Elkins Helped Shape Future," *Waco Tribune-Herald*, Nov. 14, 2009, www.wacotrib.com/sports/baylor/football/baylor-legend-elkins-helped-shape-future-of-college-football-gets/article.

87   His father was gassed . . . until I was 16.": Werner, "Baylor Legend Elkins."

87   [Elkins] drove up to campus . . . like the Real McCoys.: Werner, "Baylor Legend Elkins."

88   Phil Bennett wanted some more "football playin' fools": Max Olson, "Bennett Aiming to Make D a Baylor Tradition," *ESPN*, April 4, 2014, espn.go.com/blog/big12/post/_/id/82235/bennett-aiming-to-make-d-a-baylor-tradition.

88   Bennett's defense was charged . . . Get them the ball,": Olson, "Bennett Aiming to Make D."

88   It "was about as good as it gets on those fronts,": Olson, "Bennett Aiming to Make D."

88   On their way to the . . . on the chain-link fence.: Olson, "Bennett Aiming to Make D."

88   "I don't want to say . . . started building expectancy.: Olson, "Bennett Aiming to Make D."

89   The Baylor women started . . . the fall of 1961.: Lefever, p. 180.

89   "simply getting into a . . . play against other schools.": Helen Cho, "The Baylor University Women's Basketball Program," *Texas Monthly*, June 2005, www.texasmonthly.com/content/texas-history-101-51.

89   She simply called coach Olga Fallen: Summer Morgan, "A Baylor Bearette," *MYPlainview.com*, April 7, 2012, www.myplainview.com/sports/article.

89   "be seen clearly as the mother of Baylor's" women's intercollegiate program: Lefever, p. 180.

89   and said she wanted to . . . they played for Baylor.: Morgan, "A Baylor Bearette."

89   Pam Bowers, who took over . . . virtually ignored the program.: Cho, "The Baylor University Women's Basketball Program."

89   I just walked in there and played because I wanted to.: Morgan, "A Baylor Bearette."
90   Fans "stampeded out of . . . headlines "Bowl Bound.": John Werner, "Bowl Eligibility Only
          Footnote," *Waco Tribune-Herald*, Oct. 20, 2013, www.wacotrib.com/sports/baylor/
          football/bowl-eligibility-only-footnote-as-bears-dismantle-cyclones/article.
90   "It's big time to . . . it doesn't stop here.": Werner, "Bowl Eligibility Only Footnote."
90   If I ever accomplish . . . and go after that.: Bettinger, p. 66.
91   A disparity between the . . . Southwest Conference: Lefever, p. 43.
91   more than a dozen . . . turned the job down.: Grant Teaff, "Step of Faith Led to Most Unex-
          pected Landing Spot," *Waco Tribune-Herald*, Aug. 31, 2013, www.wacotrib.com/sports/
          baylor/football/grant-teaff-step-of-faith-led-to-most-unexpected-landing/article.
91   "My plan was to . . . what she had said.: Teaff, "Step of Faith."
91   Teaff and he were . . . accepted the job,": Teaff, "Step of Faith."
91   Teaff came to Baylor with the fervor of a revival preacher.: Lefever. p. 45.
92   "the only Moore in . . . win was his son.": Graham Hays, "Crazy Comeback Sends Baylor
          to Semis," *espnW.com*, June 1, 2014, http://espn.go.com/espnw/news-commentary-
          article/11014100/2014-ncaa-softball-tournament-baylor-bears-come-back-stun-ken-
          tucky-wildcats.
92   I won't forget that . . . forget who I am.: Hays, "Crazy Comeback Sends Baylor into Semis."
93   Some of them . . . early in the fourth quarter.: Brandon Chatmon, "Baylor Just Finds a Way
          — Again," *ESPN.com*, Oct. 12, 2014, http://espn.go.com/blog/big12/post/_/id/90803/
          baylor-just-find-a-way-again.
93   "I told our guys we weren't going to lose that game,": Chatmon, "Baylor Just Finds a Way."
93   Petty gave Callahan some . . . too nervous to watch.: "Baylor Erases 21-Point Deficit, in
          Final 11 Minutes," *ESPN.com*, Oct. 12, 2014, http://scores.espn.go.com/ncf/recap?
          gameId=400547868.
93   I don't think I . . . That's too much pressure.": "Baylor Erases 21-Point Deficit."
94   Hordes of recruiters weren't . . . his senior season: John Werner, "Hall of Fame Profile,"
          Waco Tribune-Herald, Jan. 24, 2014, www.wacotrib.com/sports/baylor/football/hall-of-
          fame-profile-all-american-qb-don-trull-took/article.
94   when Bridgers invited the . . . and doing his best.: Werner, "Hall of Fame Profile."
94   I had heard of . . . never heard of Baylor.: Werner, "Hall of Fame Profile."
95   "That was crazy,": "Terrance Ganaway Runs for 200 Yards," *ESPN*, Dec. 29, 2011, scores.
          espn.go.com/ncf/recap?fameId=313630239.
95   The game had barely . . . nation to enjoy this,": Terrance Ganaway Runs."
95   "Players were chanting, . . . He was gone.: Eatman, p. 270.
95   My advice to Baylor fans would be to let him go. It's time.: Brice Cherry, "League of Super-
          heroes has place for RG3," *Waco Tribune-Herald*, Dec. 30, 2011, www.wacotrib.com/
          sports/baylor/football/brice-cherry-league-of-superheroes-has-place-for-rg/article.

WORKS CITED

"Baylor Buries Oklahoma State for 15th Straight Home Victory." *ESPN.com*. 23 Nov. 2014, http://
          scores.espn.go.com/ncf/recap?gameId=400547896.
"Baylor Erases 21-Point Deficit in Final 11 Minutes, Stuns TCU." ESPN.com. 12 Oct. 2014. http://
          espn.go.com/ncf/recap?gameId=400547868.
"Baylor Pummels Texas Tech Even After Robert Griffin III Leaves Game." *ESPN*. 26 Nov.
          2011. scores.espn.go.com/ncf/recap?gameid=313300239.
"Baylor Survives Late Blunder, Tops Oklahoma State in OT; Cowboys Lose

Seventh Straight." *Dallas Morning News*. 17 Feb. 2014. www.dallasnews.com/sports/college-sports/baylor-bears/20140217/baylor-survives-late-blunder-tops-oklahoma-state-in-ot-cowboys-lose-seventh-straight.ece.

"Bears Shutout Defending National Champion at Arkansas." *baylorbears.com*. 6 Oct. 2006. www.baylorbears.com/sports/m-footbl/spec-rel/100606aaa.html.

Bettinger, Jim & Julie S. *The Book of Bowden*. Nashville: TowleHouse Publishing, 2001.

Blount, Luke. "Baylor Upsets No. 7 Syracuse on National Television, 35-12." *baylorbears.com*. 7 Sept. 2007. www.baylorbears.com/sports/m-footbl/spec-rel/090707aaa.html.

-----. "Bears Upset No. 12 Longhorns 34-24." *baylorbears.com*. 9 Nov. 1974. www.baylorbears.com/sports/m-footbl/spec-rel/110907aaa.html.

-----. "Ryan LaMotta Waves Off Sun Devils." *baylorbears.com*. 5 June 2007. www.baylorbears.com/sports/m-basebl/spec-rel/060507aaa.html.

Borden. Sam. "The Basketball Player's Guide to the (European) Galaxy." *New York Times*. 12 Jan. 2014. www.nytimes.com/2014/01/13/sports/basketball/the-basketball-players-guide-to-the-european-galaxy.html?_r=2.

Brown, Jeff. "Spotlight: Cyril Richardson." *baylorbears.com*. 5 Oct. 2013. baylorbears.com/sports/m-footbl/mtt/richardson_cyril00.html.

Cadena, Laura A. "Longest Softball Game to End." *The Lariat*. 14 Sept. 1995. www.baylor.edu/lariatarchives/news.php?action=story&story=8736.

Campbell, Dave. "Foreword: The Bears' Colossal Year." *Year of the Bear: The Winningest Year in College Sports History*. Waco: Pediment Publishing, 2012. 4-7.

-----. "The Legendary Texas Sportswriter Recalls Some of Baylor's Best Games of the 1950s." *baylorbears.com*. 9 Dec. 2013. www.baylorbears.com/sports/m-footbl/spec-rel/120913aab.html.

-----. "Veteran Writer Remembers Baylor Great Jack Wilson." *baylorbears.com*. 25 April 2001. www.baylorbears.com/sports/m-footbl/spec-rel/042501aaa.html.

Chatmon, Brandon. "Baylor Just Finds a Way — Again." *ESPN.com*. 12 Oct. 2014. http://espn.go.com/blog/big12/post/_.id/90803/baylor-just-finds-a-way-again.

-----. "Future Is Now for Baylor's Hall, Cannon." *ESPN.com*. 12 Sept. 2014. http://espn.com/blog/big12/post/_id/89158/future-is-now-for-baylors-hall-cannon.

Cherry, Brice. "Baylor Infielder Shrugs Off Junior Slump." *Waco Tribune-Herald*. 21 May 2010. www.wacotrib.com/sports/baylor/baylor-infielder-shrugs-off-junior-slump/article.

-----. "Baylor Lady Bears Are Swatting Everyone's Best Shot." *Waco Tribune-Herald*. 20 March 2012. www.wacotrib.com/sports/baylor/baylor-lady-bears-are-swatting-everyone-s-best-shot/article.

-----. "Griner Dunks as Lady Bears Slam Gator Jaws Shut, 76-57." *Waco Tribune-Herald*. 21 March 2012. www.wacotrib.com/sports/baylor/griner-dunks-as-lady-bears-slam-gator-jaws-shut/article.

-----. "Lady Bears' 'Miracle' Mariah Chandler Ever-Grateful for Her Life." *Waco Tribune Herald*. 21 Nov. 2012. www.wacotrib.com/sports/baylor/brice-cherry-lady-bears-miracle-mariah-chandler-ever-grateful-for/article.

-----. "League of Superheroes Has Place for RG3." *Waco Tribune-Herald*. 30 Dec. 2011. www.wacotrib.com/sports/baylor/football/brice-cherry-league-of-superheroes-has-place-for-rg/article.

-----. "No Hint of Panic in Trailing Bears." *Waco Tribune-Herald*. 17 Nov. 2013. www.wacotrib.com/sports/baylor/football/brice-cherry-no-hint-of-panic-in-trailing-bears/article.

Cho, Helen. "The Baylor University Women's Basketball Program Has Come a Long Way." *Texas Monthly*. June 2005. www.texasmonthly.com/content/texas-history-101-51.

Cunningham. Carson. "'Jackie' Robinson Back at London Games." *Real Clear History*. 23 July 2012. www.realclearhistory.com/articles/2012/07/23/jackie_robinson_back_at_london_games_30.html.

Dennis, Regina. "Heisman Winner's Superman Socks Soar in Popularity." *Year of the Bear: The Winningest Year in College Sports History*. Waco: Pediment Publishing, 2012. 27-28.

Eatman, Nick. *Art Briles Looking Up: My Journey from Tragedy to Triumph*. Chicago: Triumph Books LLC, 2013.

Fiedler, Randy. "This Week in Baylor History: The Winless Basketball Season That Would Fuel an Amazing Turnaround." *Baylor Arts & Sciences.* 18 Feb. 2013. blogs.baylor.edu/artsandsciences/2013/02/18.

Goreham, Janet. "Keeping Up with the Jones." *Sharing the Victory Magazine.* 8 May 2009. http://www.sharingthevictory.com/vsItemDisplay.1sp&obectID=AC8A85E2-99A5-4CD&.

Hawkins, Stephen. "Blind Eye No Excuse for Baylor's Isaiah Austin." *boston.com.* 13 Feb. 2014. www.boston.com/sports/colleges/mens-basketball/2014/02/13-blind-eye-no-excuse-for-baylor-isaiah-austin.

Hays, Graham. "Crazy Comeback Sends Baylor into Semis." *espnW.com.* 1 June 2014. http://espn.go.com/espnw/news-commentary-article/11014100/2014-ncaa-softball-tournament-baylor-bears-come-back-stun-kentucky-wildcats.

-----. "Makenzie, Kim Make Perfect Team." *ESPN.* 13 Feb. 2014. http://espn.go.com/womens-college-basketball/story/_/id10437949.

Henry, John. "Jack Robinson Returns to London 64 Years after Winning the Gold." *Star-Telegram.* 25 July 2012. www.star-telegram.com/2012/07/25/4126689/jack-robinson-returns-to-london.html.

-----. "Baylor Football Legend: Mike Singletary." *baylorbears.com.* 4 Oct. 2013. www.baylorbears.com/sports-m-footbl/spec-rel/100413aaa.html.

Horn, Barry. "Baylor's Kim Mulkey Is Fierce, Loving and Loyal, But Don't Get on Her Bad Side." *Dallas Morning News.* 9 March 2012. www.dallasnews.com/sports/college-sports/baylor-bears/20120309-baylor-s-kim-mulkey-is-fierce-loving-and-loyal-but-dont-get-on-her-bad-side.ece.

"The Immortal Ten." *baylorbears.com: Traditions.* baylorbears.com/trads/bay-immortal-10.html.

Lefever, Alan J. *The History of Baylor Sports.* Waco: Baylor University Press, 2013.

"Mascot History." *Baylor Bear Program.* www.baylor.edu/bear/index.php?id=18243.

Madden, Lance. "Robert Griffin III, Adidas Have a Lot of Sock Swag." *Forbes.* 21 Sept. 2012. www.forbes.com/sites/lancemadden/2012/09/21/robert-griffin-iii-adidas-have-a-lot-of-sock-swag/.

"Melissa Jones, BA '11." *Baylor Magazine.* Summer 2011. www.baylor.edu/alumni/magazine/0904/news.php?action=story&story=95855.

Morgan, Summer. "A Baylor Bearette: Lady Bears Have Come a Long Way Since Sue Turner's Tenure." *MYPlainview.com.* 7 April 2012. www.myplainview.com/sports/article.

Moss, Irv. "Colorado Classics: Legacy High Alum Melissa Jones Was an Inspirational Athlete at Baylor." *The Denver Post.* 26 Dec. 2012. www.denverpost.com/ci_22259767/legacy-high-alum-melissa-jones-was-an-inspirational.

Mulkey, Kim with Peter May. *Won't Back Down: Teams, Dreams and Family.* Philadelphia: Da Capo Press, 2007.

"Obi Leaps for Bears' 1st National Title Since 2009." *Waco Tribune-Herald.* 16 March 2014. www.wacotrib.com/sports/baylor/baylor_track_and_field/obi-leaps-for-bears-st-national-title-since/article.

"Obi Wins NCAA Indoor Triple Jump Crown." *baylorbears.com.* 15 March 2014. www.baylorbears.com/sports/c-track/recaps/031514aab.html.

Olson, Max. "Baylor Finds Breakout Weapon in Norwood." *ESPN.com.* 19 Nov. 2013. http://espn.go.com/blog/ncfnation/post/_/id?88654/baylor-finds-breakout-weapon-in-norwood.

-----. "Baylor Shouldn't Apologize for 'Ugly' Win." *ESPN.com.* 24 Nov. 2014. http://espn.go.com/blog/big12/post/_/id/93073/baylor-shouldnt-apologize-for-ugly-win.

-----. "Bennett Aiming to Make D a Baylor Tradition." *ESPN.com.* 4 April 2014. http://espn.go.com/blog/big12/post/_/id/82235/bennett-aiming-to-make-d-a-baylor-tradition.

Orts, Jason. "Baylor 75, Cal 56: Lady Bears Come Alive in 2nd Half to Advance to Sweet 16." *Waco Tribune-Herald.* 24 March 2014. www.wacotrib.com/sports/baylor/lady_bears_basketball/baylor-cal-lady-bears-come-alive-in-nd-half-to/article.

-----. "Lady Bears Freshman Nina Davis Overlooked No More." *Waco Tribune-Herald.* 9 Feb. 2014. www.wacotrib.com/sports/baylor/lady_bears_basketball/lady-bears-freshman-nina-davis-overlooked-no-more/article.

Parchman, Will. "K-State's Heisman, BCS Title Hopes Cast Aside." *Waco Tribune-Herald.* 18 Nov. 2012. www.wacotrib.com/sports/baylor/will-parchman-k-state-s-heisman-bcs-hopes-cast/article.

-----. "Ludy Saves Bears from Epic Collapse." *Waco Tribune-Herald*. 20 March 2011. www.wacotrib. com/sports/baylor/ludy-saves-bears-from-epic-collapse/article.

Partsch, Raymond A. III. "Huber Has His Family Proud to Sport Colors of Baylor Bears." *Beaumont Enterprise*. 24 Dec. 2013. www.beaumontenterprise.com/news/article/huber-has-his-family-proud-to-sport-colors-of-5090840.

Patrick, Dick. "Building Baylor Took Bit of Luck." *USA TODAY*. 5 April 2005. usatoday30.usa today.com/sports/college/womensbasketball/tourney05/2005-04-04-baylor-recruits_x.htm.

Pond, David. "Seeing the Light." *Sharing the Victory Magazine*. March/April 2012. http://archives. fca.org/vsItemDisplay.1sp?method=display.1sp?method=display&objectid=C0FF2C68-C2 9A-EE.

"Program History." *2013 Baylor Football Media Almanac*. 86-91. www.baylorbears.com/sports/m-footbl/13-media-almanac.html.

"Robert Griffin III." *baylorbears.com*. www.baylorbears.com/sports/m-footbl/mtt-griffiniii_ robert00.html.

Schlabach, Mark. "Briles' Offense Built Around Each QB." *ESPN*. 16 Oct. 2013. espn.go.com/ college-football/story/_/id/9833069/baylor-coach-art-briles-builds-offense-quarterback.

Shamik, Morton. "A Coach Even the Faculty Likes." *Sports Illustrated*. 18 Nov. 1963. sports illustrated.cnn.com/vault/article/magazine/MAG1075384/index.htm.

Sherrington, Kevin. "Late Mickey Sullivan Kept Baylor Baseball on Top with Casual Style." *Dallas Morning News*. 31 March 2012. www.dallasnews.com/sports/columnists/kevin-sherrington/20120331-sherrington-late-mickey-sullivan-kept-baylor-baseball-on-top-with-casual-style.ece.

Staples, Andy. "Fueled by Balanced Offense, Baylor Eyeing a Big 12 Title." *Sports Illustrated*. 16 April 2013. http://sportsillustrated.cnn.com/college-football/news/20130416/baylor-offense.

Teaff, Grant. "2 Seasons That Changed Baylor Football Forever." *Waco Tribune-Herald*. 22 Sept. 2013. www.wacotrib.com/sports/baylor/football/grant-teaff-seasons-that-changed-baylor-football-forever/article.

-----. "1980 Team Turned Setback into a Comeback." *Waco Tribune-Herald*. 28 Oct. 2013. www. wacotrib.com/sports/baylor/football/grant-teaff-remembers-team-turned-setback-into-a-comeback/article.

-----. "Confident Bears Showed the Difference in '72." *Waco Tribune-Herald*. 7 Sept. 2013. www. wacotrib.com/sports/baylor/football/grant-teaff-confident-bears-showed-the-difference-in/article.

-----. "Final Games End, But Memories Last." *Waco Tribune-Herald*. 7 Dec. 2013. www.wacotrib. com/sports/baylor/football/grant-teaff-remembers-final-games-end-but-memories-last/ article.

-----. "Higher Stakes Yield Cheers at 'Big House.'" *Waco Tribune-Herald*. 5 Oct. 2013. www.waco-trib.com/sports/baylor/football/grant-teaff-remembers-higher-stakes-yield-cheers-at-big-house/article.

-----. "Memories Extend Beyond Field of Play." *Waco Tribune-Herald*. 7 Nov. 2013. www.wacotrib. com/sports/baylor/football/grant-teaff-memories-extend-beyond-field-of-play/article.

-----. "Step of Faith Led to Most Unexpected Landing Spot." *Waco Tribune-Herald*. 31 Aug. 2013. www.wacotrib.com/sports/baylor/football/grant-teaff-step-of-faith-led-to-most-unexpect-ed-landing/article.

-----. "Wriggly Stunt Helps 1978 Baylor Team Turn Corner." *Waco Tribune-Herald*. 12 Oct. 2013. www.wacotrib.com/sports/baylor/football/grant-teaff-wriggly-stunt-helps-baylor-team-turn-corner/article.

"Terrance Ganaway." *baylorbears.com*. www.baylorbears.com/sports/m-footbl/mtt/ganaway_ terrance00.html.

"Terrance Ganaway Runs for 200 Yards, 5 TDs in High-Scoring Alamo Bowl." *ESPN*. 29 Dec. 2011. http://scores.espn.go.com/ncf/recap?gameId=313630239.

Torres, Pablo S. "Back of All Trades." *Sports Illustrated*. 26 Sept. 2011. sportsillustrated.cnn.com/ vault/article/magazine/MAG1190636/index.htm.

Trotter, Jake. "How the Baylor Bears Were Built." *ESPN.com*. 16 Feb. 2015. http://espn.go.com/blog/ big12/post/_/id/96172/how-the-baylor-bears-were-built.

Ubben, David. "Baylor Continuing to 'Shock' the World." *foxsports.com*. 12 Nov. 2013. msn.fox sports.com/southwest/story/baylor-continuing-to-shock-the-world-111213.

Wahl, Grant. "Choice Words." *Sports Illustrated*. 12 Dec. 2005. sportsillustrated.cnn.com/vault/article/magazine/MAG1114641/index.htm.

Watkins, Calvin. "Ordeal Brings Blackmon Sisters Closer: Near Death Last Spring, Baylor Senior Forward Is Now Full of Life." *The Dallas Morning News*. 3 April 2005. nl.newsbank.com/nl-search/we/archives?p_action=doc&p_docid=10949C3B1352B659.

Werner, John. "#4 Baylor 63, Texas Tech 34: Resilient, to Boot." *Waco Tribune-Herald*. 17 Nov. 2013. www.wacotrib.com/sports/baylor/football/baylor-texas-tech-resilient-to-boot/article.

-----. "Afterword: Redefining Unbelievable." *Year of the Bear: The Winningest Year in College Sports History*. Waco: Pediment Publishing, 2012. 139-142.

-----. "Baylor Legend Elkins Helped Shape Future of College Football, Gets Hall of Fame Nod." *Waco Tribune-Herald*. 14 Nov. 2009. www.wacotrib.com/sports/baylor/football/baylor-legend-elkins-helped-shape-future-of-college-football-gets/article.

-----. "Baylor Men Knock Off No. 3 Creighton, 85-55, to Advance to Sweet 16." *Waco Tribune-Herald*. 24 March 2014. www.wacotrib.com/sports/baylor/mens_basketball/baylor-men-knock-off-no-creighton-to-advance/article.

-----. "Baylor Overcomes No. 14 TCU in 50-48 Thriller." *Year of the Bear: The Winningest Year in College Sports History*. Waco: Pediment Publishing, 2012. 9-12.

-----. "Baylor Receiver Lets Game Do His Talking." *Waco Tribune-Herald*. 15 Oct. 2010. www.wacotrib.com/sports/football/baylor-receiver-lets-game-do-his-talking/article.

-----. "Baylor's Huber Following Father's Lead in Football, Medicine." *Waco Tribune-Herald*. 21 Sept. 2013. www.wacotrib.com/sports/football/baylor/baylors-huber-following-father-s-lead-in-football-medicine/article.

-----. "Baylor's New Era: RG3's Last-Minute Win over Oklahoma Started It All." *Waco Tribune-Herald*. 7 Nov. 2013. www.wacotrib.com/sports/baylor/football/baylor-s-new-era-rg-s-last-minute-win-over/article.

-----. "Bears Anxious to Disprove Road Woes." *Waco Tribune-Herald*. 12 Oct. 2013. www.wacotrib.com/sports/baylor/football/bears-anxious-to-disprove-road-woes/article.

-----. "Bears Rein in Mustangs with Solid Defensive Effort, 59-24." *Waco Tribune-Herald*. 3 Sept. 2012. www.wacotrib.com/sports/football/baylor/bears-rein-in-mustangs-with-solid-defensive-effort/article.

-----. "Bears Turn College Football World on Its Ear with Blowout of BCS #1 Kansas State." *Waco Tribune-Herald*. 18 Nov. 2012. www.wacotrib.com/sports/baylor/bears-turn-college-foot-ball-world-on-its-ear-with-blowout/article.

-----. "Bowl Eligibility Only Footnote as Bears Dismantle Cyclones 71-7." *Waco Tribune-Herald*. 20 Oct. 2013. www.wacotrib.com/sports/baylor/football/bowl-eligibility-only-footnote-as-bears-dismantle-cyclones/article.

-----. "DE McAllister Showing Doubters Wrong at Baylor." *Waco Tribune-Herald*. 5 Oct. 2013. www.wacotrib.com/sports/baylor/de-mcallister-showing-doubters-wrong-at-baylor/article.

-----. "Floyd Casey's 1st Tenants Share Tales of 1950 Triumphs." *Waco Tribune-Herald*. 31 Aug. 2013. www.wacotrib.com/sports/baylor/football/floyd-casey-s-st-tenants-share-tales-of-triumphs/article.

-----. "Griffin Strike with 8 Seconds Left Gives Baylor 1st-Ever Win Over Okla-homa, 45-38." *Year of the Bear: The Winningest Year in College Sports History*. Waco: Pediment Publishing, 2012. 16-19.

-----. "Grind-It-Out win for Unbeaten Baylor, 35-25." *Waco Tribune-Herald*. 13 Oct. 2013. www.wacotrib.com/sports/baylor/football/grind-it-out-win-for-unbeaten-baylor/article.

-----. "Hall of Fame Profile: All-American QB Don Trull Took Leap of Faith with Baylor." *Waco Tribune-Herald*. 24 Jan. 2014. www.wacotrib.com/sports/baylor/football/hall-of-fame-profile-all-american-qb-don-trull-took/article.

-----. "Last Year's Baylor Comeback over Kansas Still Boggles the Mind." *Waco Tribune-Herald*. 2 Nov. 2012. www.wacotrib.com/sports/baylor/john-werner-last-year-s-baylor-comeback-6.5

NAME INDEX
(LAST NAME, DEVOTION DAY NUMBER)

Aaron, Hank 49
Acy, Quincy 7, 40
Adams, E.T. 83
Alexander, Cody 71
Anderson, David 79
Angry Birds 58
Aniston, Jennifer 56
Armstead, Tre'Von 24
Ashe, Arthur 4
Austin, Isaiah 59, 85
Baker, Troy 80
Barmore, Leon 27
Baylor, Elgin 94
Bennett, Phil 21, 71, 77, 88
Berra, Yogi 38
Blackmon, Stan 46
Blackmon, Steffanie 35, 46
Blackmon, Tiffanie 46
Borden, Sam 31
Bowden, Bobby 47, 90
Bowers, Pam 89
Boyd, Sam 4, 61
Bradshaw, Wesley 6
Bridgers, John 28, 87, 91, 94
Bridges, Frank 6
Briles, Art 2, 5, 8, 11, 19, 21, 23, 24, 26, 36, 37, 39, 41, 45, 48, 50, 54, 56, 58, 60, 62, 65, 66, 69, 74, 75, 77, 80, 90, 95
Brock, Bob 44
Broxton, Jarrell 80
Broyles, Frank 42
Bryant, Bear 36, 51
Burk, Adrian 42
Burk, Billy 79
Callahan, Chris 93
Campbell, Dave 14
Campbell, Raynor 86
Candaele, Coley 71
Canion, Whitney 17
Cannon, KD 24, 77
Carpenter, Don 18
Carter, Tweety 40
Carter, Zane 33

Castellaw, Jack 55
Chafin, Devin 80, 93
Chandler, Alicia 25
Chandler, Mariah 25
Cherry, Brice 95
Chery, Kenny 70
Cinderella 64
Clements, Randy 84
Coates, Sam 6
Coleman, Bill 14
Coleman, Corey 77, 93
Cookie Monster 58
Cousin Itt 56
Crawford, Marty 67
Crockrom, Danielle 35
Csonka, Larry 79
Davis, Jordan 3
Davis, Nina 13
Dewlen, Al 14
Dillow, Sam 55
Dixon, Ahmad 16, 32, 65
Dogg, Snoop 26
Downs, Terry 18
Drango, Spencer 80
Drew, Scott 40, 59, 70, 85
Dudley, Merle 55
Duke, Deann 44
Dunn, LaceDarius 40
Eatman, Nick 23, 41, 54, 65, 74
Elam, Mickey 68
Elizabeth, Queen 57
Elizabeth, Queen II 57
Elkins, Lawrence 87
Elmo 58
Embree, Jon 61
Fallen, Olga 89
Feldman, Rudy 91
Fiedler, Randy 49
Finley, Jay 23
Florence, Nick 26, 32, 36, 39, 50, 60, 62, 66, 77
Foster, Ivey 55
Fouts, John 47
Freeman, Kirby 65
Frerking, Andrew 69

Fuller, Clay 24
Fuller, Kyle 80
Galloway, Gale 18
Ganaway, Terrance 6, 8, 36, 95
Gantt, Babe 47
Gentry, Dennis 9
George VI, King 57
Gillespie, Gordie 77
Glaze, Ralph 83
Goodley, Antwan 16, 24, 45, 93
Griffin, Robert III 11, 15, 20, 23, 24, 26, 30, 36, 39, 41, 48, 50, 58, 60, 62, 65, 66, 74, 76, 77, 95
Griner, Brittany 15, 46, 51
Gush, Jim 71
Hailey, Bob 55
Hainsfurther, Joey 81
Hamilton, R.H. 6
Haney, Jerry 79
Hannah, R.L. 55
Harbour, Todd 10, 11, 22
Harris, Ron 9
Harts, Trey 10
Hawkins, Ari 92
Hayden, Kimetria 51
Hefley, Riley 83
Henderson, Bill 14, 49
Heslip, Brady 70
Hicks, Mike 48, 50
Hogg, Sonja 89
Holl, Holly 17, 92
Holl, Sam 50
Huber, Stefan 75
Isbell, Larry 18, 53
Jefferson, Cory 59
Jeffrey, Neal 12
Jennings, Morley 61
Jones, Aaron 20, 48, 69
Jones, Melissa 73
Jones, Nichole 22
Joy 53
Kelly, James Clyde "Abe" 55

![BEARS](header image)

Kent, Phillip 12
Kettler, Kelsi 17
Kittrell, Kit 14
Lackey, Eddie 50, 71
Lady 53
Lambert, Sheila 35
LaMotta, Ryan 33
Landrith, Robin 92
Leach, Mike 74
Lebby, Jeff 8
Lefever, Alan J. 1, 29, 38, 49, 55, 72, 91
Letterman, David 58
Linwood, Shock 24, 56, 69, 77
Little, Floyd 79
Ludy, Josh 81
Martin, Glasco 32, 37, 39, 56, 69
McAllister, Chris 21
McCall, Abner 42
McCaw, Ian 11, 15, 54
McCreery, Scotty 69
McDermott, Doug 70
Middleton, Darryl 31
Miller, Jake 81
Mitchell, Clint 87
Moore, Glenn 93
Morriss, Guy 11
Muir, Blake 80
Mulkey, Kim 3, 13, 27, 35, 63, 73
Muncy, Max 81
Murray, W.E. 55
Navjar, Jordan 48
Nevitt, Chuck 42
Norwood, Brian 45
Norwood, Levi 2, 16, 24, 45, 69
Nowlin, Jeanne 89
Obi, Felix 10
O'Brien, Davey 61
O'Neal, Shaquille 69

O'Neale, Royce 70
Palmer, Lindsay 73
Parchman, Will 32
Parker, Dudley 42
Patterson, Billy 61
Patterson, Gary 34
Patterson, Jack 91
Pawelek, Joe 9
Perlman, Jonathan 67
Petty, Bryce 2, 16, 30, 37, 50, 56, 60, 62, 66, 69, 77, 88, 90, 93
Pipes, Greg 79
Pitt, Brad 56
Reese, Tevin 20, 37, 45, 69, 77
Richardson, Cyril 69, 84
Roberts, Jennifer 35
Robertson, Makenzie 63
Robinson, Jackie 49, 57
Royal, Darrell 35
Russell, Seth 69
Ruth, Babe 49
Salubi, Jarred 8
Sauer, George 4, 53
Schembechler, Bo 34
Schlabach, Mark 66
Scott, Chameka 35
Seastrunk, Lache 32, 39, 56, 77
Shamik, Morton 28
Sherrington, Kevin 67
Simpson, Lanear 48
Sims, Odyssey 78
Singletary, Mike 9, 54
Skinner, Brian 7
Slater, Chris 81
Smith, Jason 5, 19, 76
Smith, Scott 64
Smith, Sarah 92
Smith, Steve 33, 43
Snider, Suzie 89
Southall, Terry 79
SpongeBob SquarePants

58
Stearns, Heather 92
Stewart, Martha 26
Strickland, Jordan 92
Sullivan, Mickey 67
Superman 58
Szymanski, Blake 36
Taylor, Phil 36
Taylor, Trooper 64
Teaff, Donell 91
Teaff, Grant 9, 12, 34, 43, 52, 54, 64, 68, 82, 91
Thomas, Frank 72
Thompson, Ricky 12
Thumann, Kaitlyn 92
Trotter, Jake 77
Trull, Don 87, 94
Turner, Sue 89
Tyson, Mike 2
Unitas, Johnny 94
VanAllen, Cory 33
Vitek, Cristin 17
Wabara, Abiola 35
Walker, James 55
Washam, Weir 55
Watkins, Danny 5
Werner, John 20
Whitaker, Chelsea 3, 35
Williams, Destiny 51
Williams, Joe 20
Williams, Terrance 20, 30, 48, 77
Wilson, Danielle 46
Wilson, Jack 14
Winchester, William 55
Wolf, Ralph 55
Woodruff, Bob 6, 18, 42
Woods, Kyle 43
Wright, Kendall 30, 48, 76, 77
Young, Paula 44
Young, Sophia 35
Young, Taylor 77

SCRIPTURES INDEX
(by DEVOTION DAY NUMBER)

Acts 1:1-14	60	Isaiah 35	22
Acts 1:15-25	35	Isaiah 53	8
Acts 2:1-21	5		
Acts 2:40-47	7	James 1:13-18	4
Acts 5:29-42	78	James 2:14-26	51
Acts 9:1-22	92	James 4:13-17	46
Acts 19:11-20	47		
		Job 1, 2:1-10	55
2 Chronicles 7:11-22	48	Job 28	19
1 Corinthians 11:17-29	49	John 1:43-51	56
		John 2:1-11	81
2 Corinthians 1:3-7	14	John 4:1-15	23
2 Corinthians 5:1-10	45	John 6:60-69	11
		John 8:12-32	42
Daniel 3	82	John 13:33-38	18
		John 19:25-30	63
Deuteronomy 30:15-20	21	John 20:1-10	41
Exodus 3:13-20	69	1 John 1:5-10	66
Exodus 20:1-17	77		
Exodus 3:1-12	54	Joshua 3	17
Ezra 3	86	Judges 6:11-23	24
Galatians 5:16-26	15	1 Kings 4:29-34; 11:1-6	36
		1 Kings 10:1-10, 18-29	31
Genesis 1, 2:1-3	1		
Genesis 7	9	2 Kings 2:1-12	6
Genesis 9:1-7	68		
Genesis 18:1-15	71	Luke 3:1-22	75
Genesis 37:1-11	58	Luke 6:20-26	10
		Luke 9:57-62	85
Hebrews 3:7-19	20	Luke 13:1-9	73
Hebrews 12:14-17	72	Luke 13:31-35	12
		Luke 15:1-10	16
Isaiah 8:11-9:7	26	Luke 18:1-8	25
		Luke 19:1-10	13

BEARS

Luke 23:26-43	43		
Luke 24:1-12	64	Philippians 2:1-11	44
Mark 3:31-35	87	1 Peter 1:3-12	90
Mark 4:35-41	2		
Mark 5:1-20	57	Psalm 18:1-6, 20-29	29
Mark 7:1-13	88	Psalm 33:1-15	34
Mark 14:66-72	59	Psalm 42	65
		Psalm 102	89
Matthew 3	50	Psalm 121	78
Matthew 4:18-22	94	Psalm 139:1-18	53
Matthew 5:38-42	37		
Matthew 6:19-24	91	Revelation 19:11-21	83
Matthew 7:7-11	27	Revelation 21:22-27; 22:1-6	30
Matthew 11:27-30	80	Revelation 22:1-17	95
Matthew 12:33-37	3		
Matthew 16:13-17	70	Romans 6:3-11	38
Matthew 24:15-31	61	Romans 11:25-36	79
Matthew 24:36-51	40	Romans 12:1-2	74
Matthew 28:1-10	32	Romans 13:8-14	67
Matthew 28:16-20	33	Romans 14:1-12	76
		Romans 14:13-23	39
Nahum 1:3-9	52		
		1 Samuel 3:1-18	62
Nehemiah 8:1-12	28		
		2 Samuel 12:1-15a	93
Numbers 13:25-14:4	84		